Audio Book Breakthrough

AUDIO BOOK BREAKTHROUGH

A Guide to Selection and Use in Public Libraries and Education

Preston Hoffman
and
Carol H. Osteyee

GREENWOOD PRESS
Westport, Connecticut · London

nsin

Library of Congress Cataloging-in-Publication Data

Hoffman, Preston Jones.
    Audio book breakthrough : a guide to selection and use in public
libraries and education / Preston Hoffman and Carol H. Osteyee.
      p.   cm.
    Includes bibliographical references (p.) and index.
    ISBN 0–313–28690–6 (alk. paper)
    1. Libraries—United States—Special collections—Talking books.
2. Public libraries—United States.   3. Sound recordings in
education. I. Osteyee, Carol H. II. Title.
Z688.T34H64   1994
025.2′882—dc20   93–1701

British Library Cataloguing in Publication Data is available.

Library of Congress Catalog Card Number: 93–1701
ISBN: 0–313–28690–6

First published in 1994

Greenwood Press, 88 Post Road West, Westport, CT 06881
An imprint of Greenwood Publishing Group, Inc.

Printed in the United States of America

The paper used in this book complies with the
Permanent Paper Standard issued by the National
Information Standards Organization (Z39.48–1984).

10 9 8 7 6 5 4 3 2 1

Contents

Tables

Glossary

The following terms are used in this work.

abridged: most common term for a less than complete version of a book or audio book

airpak: packaging made of styrofoam covered with paper that is used for audio books

audio book: term for book on cassette, phonograph record, or compact disc; has the advantage of not being copyrighted; the term now generally used by the industry

audio script: the text used by a reader to create an audio book; may be the book itself or an original work, but is most often an abridgment

automatic dialogue replacement or ADR: the practice in film of having one actor's voice replace all the words spoken by another actor; actors who work in ADR also often interpret audio books

book jobbers: book distributors

bookpak: packaging made of heavy-duty cardboard covered with plastic that is used for audio books and preferred by libraries

Books on Tape: the copyrighted name of a California corporation that is commonly used as a generic name for complete audio books

bridges: a section added to an abridged audio book that did not appear in the text but was necessary to connect sections of the original in order to make sense of the abridged version

compact disc: a CD-ROM devoted to sound, whether music or audio book

complete: a synonym for unabridged, that is, containing the entire work, especially as in a complete audio book

condensation: the practice of abridging a book in a manner that changes the prose appreciably, as contrasted to excerpting a book

data compression: the process of speeding up the performance of a work by crowding together discrete units of sound, resulting in a faster reading without pitch change

Data Discman: copyrighted name for a Sony Corporation personal computer for Talking Type books on CD-ROM

diffracted: a term used in the industry for abridged books

dramatic rights: legal permission to create and perform a drama based upon a book, as distinguished from reading rights

dramatization: a type of production that implies the use of multiple voices and certain changes in text; in a complete audio book the "he said, she said's" are retained; in a true dramatization, whether for radio or otherwise, they are dropped. Sound effects are also more usual in dramatized versions, though they also appear in some complete audio books.

ephemera: a library term for materials that have a very short life span

excerpting: the practice of creating an audio book by recording discrete units from a book, as in selecting certain short stories from a collection

flat character: a character in an audio book who is given an unvoiced interpretation

full voice or fully voiced: the practice by which the reader of an audio book creates a unique vocal characterization for each person

hot link: a type of keyword searching that allows a computer user to move easily from one keyword to another

hypertext: a form of fiction in which a reader using a computer creates a personalized book in conjunction with the work of an author

interpretation: used as a synonym for reading, as in describing an actor's performance while creating an audio book

looping: a synonym for Automatic Dialogue Replacement

partially voiced: the practice by which the reader gives only some of the characters of an audio book distinct vocal characterizations

performance literature: oral interpretation of literature primarily recorded

producer: a synonym for publisher, but sometimes used in audio as being more appropriate for a nonprint format

publishers: companies that create and sell books; although the term producer may be preferred in dealing with audio, the companies, especially those that are part of larger book-oriented corporations, seem to prefer publisher.

reading rights: legal permission to create and distribute an audio book, generally purchased from a book's print publisher or its author

repak: the variety of cardboard cases, sometimes enclosing plastic Norelco cases, in which abridged audio books generally are packaged; usually replaced for library use *round character:* a character in an audio book who is given a fully voiced interpretation

sampling: a music industry technique used in some audio books whereby small aural units are expanded into sound effects

scrolling: the process of moving text up or down on a computer screen

semivoiced: same as partially voiced

Talking Books: the copyrighted name for audio books produced by the Library of Congress; a common term for complete audio books

Talking Type: copyrighted name for a Sony Corporation CD-ROM book played on the Data Discman

unabridged book on cassette tape: a synonym for complete audio books, too clumsy to be used often; Books on Tape claims that its copyright covers any use of this term or any variation upon it

unvoiced: the practice by which the reader of an audio book maintains one vocal style for all characters

vanity audio: a portion of the audio business in which authors pay producers to create audio books from their works; especially common in self-help titles

voiced: the practice by which the reader of an audio book gives a character a distinct interpretation

Walkman: the copyrighted name for a Sony Corporation personal tape player; often used generically

CHAPTER *1*

An Introduction to Audio Books

The electronic audio book has broken through as a new entertainment and educationai medium, as a profitable business, as a gateway to other varieties of electronic books, and as a very popular library service. A 1991 study indicated that the polled libraries spent about 6 percent of their materials-purchasing budgets on audio, averaging $13,000 per library. Larger libraries spent the highest proportion, about 8 percent.[1] Indeed, audio budgets are increasing for many libraries at a time when funds for acquisition of other materials are stagnant.[2] Yet collection development and audio visual librarians have few sources of information to guide their choices; available sources tend to be incomplete in their coverage, to have unknown evaluation standards, and often to be influenced by the advertising dollars upon which they depend. This book attempts to meet this need for information by examining audio books in general, evaluating the available sources, abstracting reviews from these sources, and suggesting selection standards.

We will deal with many unresolved difficulties with audio books, including establishing the relative value of the complete and the abridged formats, identifying the best sources, formulating a rationale for audio book acquisition by public libraries, creating acceptable policies for establishing collections, measuring demand, and studying how audio books can be used in education and for adult literacy.

Chapter 1 is also an overview of the history of audio books and includes a rationale for their inclusion in library collections. Our information comes from our varied experience with audio. Preston Hoffman, Extension Services Librarian for the Burke County (NC) Library System and Librarian at Valdese Public Library, is the *Book Sounds* columnist for the *Wilson Library Bulletin* and a past contributor to the *Library Journal.* Carol Osteyee, Ed.D., has developed curricula for public schools, colleges, and literacy programs, has been a college professor, and is currently a classroom teacher at George Hildebrand Elementary School, in Burke County. Kathi Sippen is Audio-Visual Librarian at Durham County (NC) Public Library and has been responsible for selecting and maintaining their collection of more than 1,000 audio titles.

Chapter 2 is a discussion of the relationship of abridged and complete or unabridged works, especially in library collections. Chapter 3, written by Sippen, discusses the theory and practice of establishing and maintaining a large library collection. In Chapter 4 Osteyee explores the selection and use of audio materials in the public schools, principally from the perspective of the classroom teacher. In Chapter 5 we share the results of a questionnaire completed by 43 public librarians involved in audio. This questionnaire solicited opinions on six topics concerning audio books in libraries: quality of the reading, sound fidelity and technical quality, durability under use, suitability of the original packaging, price in relation to other producers, and replacement policy. The plethora of different vendors, many of whom handle each others' products (and add a surcharge to the price of their source either directly or by eliminating discounts), seems to be one of the barriers which has prevented this format from becoming more available generally. Many librarians who have been acquiring audio books for a considerable length of time have information about the producers and distributors that could be valuable to those just beginning a collection. Chapter 6 is an annotated bibliography of outstanding titles, both complete and abridged, mostly for adults. Chapter 7 is a directory of audio book producers and distributors, compiled via questionnaire, that includes discussion of the strengths and weaknesses of the best-known producers and distributors.

HISTORY AND DEVELOPMENT

The audio book completes a full circle begun more than 5,000 years ago when previously oral poetry was transcribed, creating the first written literature. Since these first records were made, improvements in technology have allowed progressively greater fidelity. The first attempts to record vocal interpretations of literature made use of the best available machinery to reproduce authors and actors doing their star turns. Today these attempts from the eras of the phonograph record are of little interest except to collectors and historians.

Even after the introduction of long-playing records and reel-to-reel tapes, what was available commercially was mostly recordings of drama, poetry, short stories, and excerpts from longer works. The best-known companies, Caedmon, Spoken Arts, Listening Library, and Halverson, usually followed either the abridged or the short-form pattern. However, complete audio books had been available commercially since at least 1957, when Libraphone published Commander William Anderson's *Nautilus Ninety North* on 16 rpm phonograph records. Libraphone, founded by the late Anthony Ditlow, was the corporate precursor of Listening Library. Mr. Ditlow was blind, but he thought audio books would also be of interest to the sighted.

The British Broadcasting Company (BBC) and, in the United States, Mind's Eye adapted fiction for radio, often drawing on children's classics. The BBC and some university radio stations in the United States also broadcast single-voice readings of classic fiction without causing too much stir. However, longer works could (and can) be obtained by the visually disabled from the United States Library of Congress, Division for the Blind and Physically Handicapped.

Not until the introduction of the cassette tape in the early 1960s was a medium suitable for full-length, complete books in general use. Even though this medium was intended originally for the spoken word, the popularity of music cassettes and the resulting ubiquity of the cassette player (especially the portable Walkman and the car tape machine) have been largely responsible for the creation of conditions favoring the sudden growth of interest in audio books.

During the 1970s two institutions contributed considerably to growing interest in audio books. The first is the Books on Tape Corporation, founded by Duvall Hecht. Since its first releases in 1975, the company has made audio books available for rental to individuals. Through an extensive advertising campaign, Books on Tape has brought this medium wide visibility, to the extent that its copyrighted name has become synonymous with the medium. Although Books on Tape can take credit for the idea of renting audio books through the mails, the company followed other producers into library sales.

The second major contributor is public radio, which made available to its listeners certain programs, especially "Radio Reader," which encouraged the habit of listening to prose readings. The reader is Dick Estelle, of Michigan State University. Mr. Estelle began reading in 1965, having inherited the basic format from his predecessor at Michigan State. He was trained in announcing and engineering rather than theater. He soon determined that newly published books were the major attraction for his audience and has continued his readings of current fiction and nonfiction ever since. In 1970 the program was syndicated and now serves over 110 radio stations. He has always read the books in full and confesses to being "repulsed by abridged books in any form."[3] The whole appeal of audio books is a mystery to Mr. Estelle. "How I can retain the interest of a listener for 28 consecutive minutes is almost beyond my comprehension. I do feel, however, that the success of my program is due to an age-old human characteristic: people love to hear stories. Whether it's over the back fence, in a bar, over the telephone, at the grocer's, or at church; whether it's gossip, factual, or dirty (or all three), people will listen to a story."[4]

Without a doubt Mr. Estelle has been left behind stylistically by the influx of professional actors trained to immerse themselves in a story and its characters and bring it and them to life. The best known of these, Frank Muller, goes so far as to say, "If you're not an actor you haven't a prayer in doing this kind of work."[5] These actors have created a new art form, one that derives from the theater but is not the same as a dramatization.

After the complete audio book began to gain in popularity in the late 1970s, several other companies entered the market. The best known of these are Recorded Books and Chivers Audio Books. Recorded Books began in 1979 in unabashed imitation of Books on Tape but soon diverged from their model. The most important innovation that Recorded Books introduced to this country was the integrated production team. Working with a professional actor in a state-of-the-art studio they are able consistently to produce a quality product. In contrast, Books on Tape, which began and remains primarily in the business of distributing rather than producing audio books, continues to offer recordings of extremely variable quality. Many of its master tapes are bought from smaller producers, and others are recorded in home studios in a lightly supervised fashion.

The signature reader for Books on Tapes, Dan Grace, who also reads as Wolfram Kandinsky, has done some excellent work but has never improved upon his early instinctive and mostly unvoiced style. Frank Muller, on the other hand, developed a breathy but uniquely emotive style for Recorded Books during the 1980s. Mr. Muller reads very little now, but many of his later works will no doubt survive as models of craftsmanship combined with inspiration.

In 1980, in Britain, Chivers Audio Books began releasing complete audio. From the beginning they consulted with librarians. Chivers perceived libraries as the primary market from the beginning and asked librarians about technique, format, and packaging. For example, librarians told Chivers that they felt fiction, especially mystery titles, would be most popular in public libraries. Chivers has now purchased John Curley & Associates and established Chivers, North America and is distributing its own products. This will allow titles deemed undesirable by G. K. Hall and either never before previously available or out of print to become available. British audio books have been prominent in U.S. libraries because listeners find that interpretations from Chivers are of considerably higher quality than most produced in the United States.

Even the oldest recordings are at least partially voiced, and many are full voice. There are several reasons for this quality. Tom Beeler, president of Chivers, NA says, "There is a much stronger British tradition of reading books as an occupation. Also, British acting puts more emphasis on interpretation by voice."[6]

In the mid to late 1980s several other innovative companies entered the fray. Blackstone Audio, formerly known as Classics on Tape, is one of the best known. The name change was the result of the vigorous defense by Duvall Hecht of his trademark, Books on Tape. At first Blackstone mostly distributed versions from older producers, especially JimCin. These were not the most creative or daring works available. Now, however, Blackstone is producing its own products and has produced some very good works, though they are still better known for low prices and interesting titles than for high technical and aesthetic standards.

Books in Motion is another notable example of a company that began with out-of-copyright classics but soon developed a unique outlook. The company is the only publisher of original, unpublished manuscripts of novels in audio form. The owner of Books in Motion, Gary Challender, was unhappy with the royalties demanded by East Coast publishers for audio versions of even moderately successful books. Then authors and agents began sending him manuscripts. "As I read some of the books coming out of New York and some of the unpublished manuscripts, I realized these manuscripts are every bit as good. Now why do I need these New York books? They aren't better literature, they are just better marketed. So I did a little experiment. Now I've got people telling me M. & M. Lehman are as good as Louis L'Amour."[7] Challender, who personally enjoys Westerns, has also made an effort to make his company a center for recording fiction about the West.

Speculation has arisen that the audio book may be a bridge to the wide use of electronic books. No one expects the electronic book to become the dominant medium overnight. However, Nathaniel Lande, an adjunct professor at the School of Journalism and Mass Communication of the University of North Carolina at Chapel Hill, has written. "Our studies indicate that the reader will adapt in a series of stages. A taste for electronic access to fiction will probably arise by way of the audio element: as the growth of books on tape has so convincingly shown, the pleasures of being read to are addictive."[8]

An innovative company that has made Lande's prediction a reality in less than a year is the Brilliance Corporation. Brilliance has been fearless in spending money to obtain the rights to best-sellers and other popular works and has been an innovator in technical matters as well. All its recent tapes use data-compression techniques in order to speed up the readings, and often the actor's voices are altered electronically in order to simulate phone calls, telepathic communication, or memories. The company drew considerable attention in 1992 with its co-development project with Sony Corp. Some Brilliance titles, known as Talking Type books, are available on the special CD-ROM used by the Sony Data Discman. As company president Mike Snodgrass explains, "You can read the text on screen, listen to the audio, or a combination of both. It shows you a page of text, reads it out loud and brings the next page up. And of course this system adds database style search and recall." The system also features instant return to the last-read page, continuous or page scrolling, 30 characters of text horizontally and 10 lines vertically, keyword search, topic search, and a hot-link system for accessing additional text or graphics. Bundled with each Sony Data Discman DD-10EXB is a CD-ROM containing a Talking Type book. Anachronistically, a group-recording technique was used to simulate the venerable radio group reading for the first title, *Sliver,* by Ira Levin. The reader uses headphones or an additional amplifier-speaker component in order to listen to the reading. The anticipated market is indicated by the inclusion of two business oriented titles among the first six titles available. Though Mr. Snodgrass identifies this product as accessible to people of limited means, the hardware is quite expensive ($549.00 as of this writing). However the software is not unreasonable, with one disc at $34.95 and two disc packages $39.95 (as of this writing).

Another innovator is Spencer Library. Rick Spencer is a public library trustee, author, screenwriter, and producer. Spencer found he had access to artists with unique abilities and decided to create a special kind of audio book. It is common in movies to use dialog replacement artists or automatic dialog replacement (ADR) to dub in speech (also known as looping) for an actor who looks the part but just can't get the voice quality needed. Replacement actors are experienced in submerging their own personalities in service to artistic collaboration.

Spencer blends acoustic music (by selected players from the Chicago Symphony Orchestra), sampling techniques, and synthesized sounds to create an original electronic score. Spencer says, "Our artists tend to be very accomplished musicians who can play guitars and violin but when they get to the MIDI synthesizer, they try to create sounds which have never been heard before by combining electronics with some existing sounds."[9] The final result is a work that can be listened to as literature, music, or pure sound. These works are available on cassette tape, CD-ROM, and soon on the special CD used by the Data Discman. The Data Discman screen will not scroll text, but will give additional visuals to enhance the listening experience.

Of course there are now many other audio book producers, some of whose products are quite good and less expensive than Books on Tape and Recorded Books. These are listed with brief commentary in Chapter 7.

AESTHETICS AND STYLE

In a pamphlet published by the Library of Congress, *The Reader–Viewer–Listener,* Lester Asheim has probed the differences among various media. According to Dr. Asheim, it is necessary to be extensively exposed to any medium in order to "appreciate its capacity to convey additional levels of meaning, and to comprehend not only the literal message but the nuances that are embedded in its manner of presentation." [10] It seems obvious that librarians and others who dismiss the significance and artistic worth of the audio book have not usually taken the time to listen carefully. Dr. Asheim says, "Listening is as much a form of learning as reading, and if you don't get the meaning at the first exposure, try, try again." [11]

Audio books may be taken more seriously in Britain than in the United States. I have come to believe this is the case not only because of testimony from British actors and listeners but also because of internal stylistic evidence. The British productions boast a consistency of style not found in this country. Conversely they also tend to be less creative. American readers sometimes try for more extensive characterization than they are capable of bringing off, which has disastrous results from an aesthetic point of view. On the other hand, Chivers's interpreters seem to use very similar techniques, usually with good if not great results. This consistency comes from the reading tradition and from strong direction and editing in the studio.

However, the British readers do not take many risks in their style of reading. They tend to stay within relatively narrow bounds as far as their vocal creativity is concerned. The emphasis tends to be upon character rather than emotion. American readers tend to be more expressive, often at the cost of weaker character development. There is no shortage of talent in the United States, but the cult of personality that has dominated the large and small screens in this country has been detrimental to the development of actors with great range. The tradition of the character actor so important to British theater and film has never been strong in the United States, and in most cases character actors here usually specialize in one eccentric type.

Certainly there is room for all of these styles and aesthetics. As Asheim has written, "We may use one medium for one kind of satisfaction and others for different kinds; and we may be able to distinguish, within a single medium, a sufficient variety of content to satisfy a great variety of needs, touch upon a great number of levels of fulfillment, and appeal to a wide range of sensibilities and expectations."[12] Some assume that audio books are merely a form of entertainment for those too busy and probably too lazy to read. But listening to and understanding an audio book that may last for ten or more hours make demands on the intellect that are comparable with reading a book. Certainly, the reels turn by themselves and the listeners need not follow the words with their eyes, but if they fail to pay attention the book soon ceases to make any sense. This is especially true with fiction.

Whereas a reader who has forgotten the name of an important character can thumb back and find this information easily, listeners quickly learn that they must remember names and other details in order to appreciate audio books. In some cases listening may make a confusing book more clear. I found that, though I had read *Wuthering Heights* several times, I understood it better after I listened because I was forced to keep the characters and the familial relationships in mind throughout. No doubt I have improved my ability in this respect through practice.

Many times the interpretation of a book by a reader will clear up details that were incomprehensible on the page. I found the slang of Evelyn Waugh's smart set opaque until I heard British readers give it the proper inflection and provide the requisite nuances. Many nineteenth-century British and American books can be more easily understood by the ear than by the eye.

The most natural way to take in words is not through the eye, but though the ear. The listener can sometimes reach a state in which every word takes on a life of its own and the story seems to enter the brain effortlessly. What's more, when I read I hear the voice of the author in my head. But when I listen, and the voices are already heard, I see the characters and the locales with a clarity which is rarely if ever reached when reading.

A good reader ceases to be one person, and each character voice takes on a life of its own, providing the opportunity for a willing suspension of disbelief that is never in my experience reached with any other medium. Expert interpreters use pace and other variations in vocal quality to bring the work to life. Finally, listeners can control what they hear by turning off the tape in order to contemplate what they have heard or by rewinding in order to clarify their first impressions.

READING STYLES

In examining audio books, the question arises of the quality and type of the reading. The earliest recorded books in this country, produced on long-playing records by the Library of Congress, tended to be very flat readings with little affect. Some recordings created according to this aesthetic are still being sold, often, though not always, at very low prices. More recently the best single-voice recordings (as opposed to multivoice recordings with a cast of actors) tend to feature a virtuoso professional actor who not only reads fiction with great sensitivity and feeling but also performs each character with a unique voice.

An example is the version of *Huckleberry Finn* read by Tim Behrens for Books in Motion. Near the end, when Tom Sawyer's mother and his aunt are trying to figure out the crazy trick that has been played on them, Mr. Behrens gives them the same vocal quality, but different accents. After all, one lives in the upper Mississippi River valley and one in the lower. It is a masterful use of technique that not only pleases the ear but also allows the listener to distinguish effortlessly between the sisters.

In some audio books, certain characters have individual voices but others do not. Often the main protagonist(s) are individualized, but other times the reader distinguishes among all the characters of his or her own sex and reads the opposite sex in a monotone. I have listened to more than one recording in which the minor characters received distinct voices, but the most important characters were read only for feeling and understanding. Using the analogy of single and multivoiced recordings, I propose that the older, flat form of narration be called *unvoiced,* that a narration with some characters individualized be called *semivoiced* or *partially voiced,* and that the completely rendered versions be called *full voice* or *fully voiced.* These terms are used throughout this book.

It may be difficult to persuade publishers to provide information about reading styles in their catalogs, as these categories are to some extent subjective—and, of course, all would have us believe that their products are of the highest quality. However, some publishers are already using the term *full voice,* and librarians and users will at least be able to discuss the various techniques.

Across these categories, the readers seem to be of two types. The first type relies upon spontaneity. Feeling that any full-length novel is too long to plan completely, this reader establishes the major voices and then reads and improvises, relying upon passion and training to create a coherent whole. The second type of reader is more deliberate and often works with shorter fiction, including children's books. This type of reader plans the tempo and tone of each scene and establishes a voice for every character. Without a doubt the most popular reader of the first type is Frank Muller, who is also the most senior and prolific reader for Recorded Books, with some 85 books. Mr. Muller studied drama and theater arts at the North Carolina School of the Arts and is a veteran of regional and off-Broadway theater. But that doesn't mean he takes the work lightly. Mr. Muller says, "It really is acting, obviously; you're playing all the characters and it's quite a load, plus the narrative text of the book, and you have to make snap decisions constantly." [13] He is best known for the emotional depth of his readings. Because he is confident in his craft, he is able to just let go before the microphone.

> The thing about being an actor, once you have the technical aspects in hand, you have to forget about them and rely upon your instincts. And if you have good performing instincts you'll make the right decisions. It's more interesting if it's subtler. You try to invest the character with a physical identity. It informs the character vocally: I change physically and I assume the character totally. The human ear picks up everything, it's astonishing. [14]

Muller is not just a natural. Like many actors, he is an intellectual, and his favorite authors are Ford Madox Ford and Joseph Conrad. He has thought deeply about his work. "This medium has a great validity in itself. I believe it's a rebirth of storytelling, in a modern way." [15]

Another reader known for her spontaneity is Sandra Burr of the Brilliance Corporation. Burr's background is very different from Frank Muller's. She can best be described as a semiprofessional actor, though she has worked in community theater since age six and has a degree in speech with a concentration in radio and TV. She studied oral interpretation but says, "I don't use it, at least not consciously." [16] One thing that she and Muller have in common is that they don't listen to competitors.

Burr is perhaps best known for her readings of Jean Auel's *Children of the Earth* series. Asked about her method she explained: "I read the book and highlight each line of text, yellow for Ayla and Green for Jondalar. The rest of the characters are just a matter of pitch and voice quality. When a character's moods change I try to think differently. Then I wing it, there is just too much material to prepare. I even improvise the songs." In this case the reading of the book required the cooperation of the author. As Burr says, "There aren't any Neolithic lexicons. I talked with Jean Auel on the phone. We recorded her pronunciations of her original words. Jean listened to the reading and gave her approval." [17]

Sometimes the author is not available for consultation, and the reader must fall back on other sources. A classic example is Recorded Books version of *The Lord of the Rings*. To avoid mistakes in the 53-hour recording, "We consulted a woman who had written her Ph.D. dissertation on the Elvish languages," Sandy Spencer, vice-president of Recorded Books relates. "She could recite from memory all three verses of Galadriel's 'Farewell Song.' I didn't even know anyone spoke

Elvish."[18] Henry Trentman of Recorded Books says, "Having authors involved in the process of making a audio book is a mixed blessing at best. In one case a female author wanted her biography of a woman read by a man. Authors have preconceived notions of how a book should be read."[19]

An example of the second kind of reader is Laurie Klein, a reader for Books in Motion. Her technique is much more painstaking and deliberate. "I begin by reading the work, paying special attention to how it makes me feel, and looking for all the clues in the text about the characters. What is their age, sex, temperament, attitude toward life? How do they relate to others? Are they round or flat? Do they speak in dialect? Based on these clues, I then determine basic voice variables for each one as a springboard for development. These include pitch, rate, quality and volume. Characters who interact often need to be easily distinguished and interesting. Perhaps the most challenging task is to play numerous characters of the same sex and age conversing."

Muller and Klein would agree in many respects, however. Both try to climb into the story and feel with each character. Both not only act with their voices but also physically enter the world of the book. Klein says, "I always visualize, I gesture, I make faces, I shift my posture, I sometimes 'look' at the imagined listener, or perhaps I change all my muscle sensing."[20]

One way to distinguish between the two types of readers is by their attitude toward mistakes. Reading up to 15 pages an hour, usually three hours a day, Muller says, "I usually blow it a couple of times a page. If you're pushing the edge of the envelope with characterizations, you're going to make mistakes. If you're not doing that you're going to bore me to tears. You have to make the characters bold and real and human."[21] Sandy Spencer, vice president of Recorded Books and an excellent reader himself, approves of this style. "Mistakes may necessitate a lot of patching in the editing room, but they're still preferable to impeccable readings. Frank and the good readers take risks, so they make a lot of errors, but we recommend that they take these risks, because only by making mistakes will they be putting their performances on the edge, providing something that's exciting and original."[22]

Tim Behrens is another very structured reader. Like his co-worker Laurie Klein, he plans in great detail. "I learned my lesson when I had to read *War of the Worlds* twice, and I never want that to happen again. That book is a study in constantly rising action, and I started too fast and by the time I was halfway through, I had no place to go."[23]

An interesting variation is the vanity audio. Toni Boyle, self-proclaimed Empress of Audio, is now working for Cassette Productions

Unlimited, who contract to produce recordings by motivational and inspirational speakers for sale at their lectures. The making and marketing of these tapes can be a tricky business. Boyle once fielded a call from an irate customer who had "bought 75 of our tapes and wanted to know why he wasn't rich yet. I told him I have listened to every tape several times, and I'm certainly not rich. If I was I wouldn't be spending the winter in Chicago." Boyle now lives in California. She says, "Audio is the most intimate medium. There is nothing to color your judgement. I teach people to be very small and close and talk with one person." [24]

LIBRARY USE

The complete or unabridged audio book has found a place in most larger public libraries. According to a *Publishers Weekly* survey, 90 percent of public libraries have audio tapes and 84 percent have spoken-word fiction and nonfiction in their collections. [25] These collections average 35 percent complete books and 65 percent abridged. Still, many libraries have resisted providing this service or provide it at a patently inadequate level for reasons ranging from lack of space and low perceived demand to charges that the medium is inherently elitist. [26] It may be useful here to outline the reasons that the establishment and maintenance of such a collection is a valuable asset to communities and libraries alike, with emphasis on the needs of the public library.

That an imbalance exists seems clear, because interest in this format is very high among members of the general public who have begun to buy, rent, and borrow tapes, yet it is somewhat less pronounced among professional working librarians. The total contribution of the American Library Association to the study of audio books has been two panel discussions during the 1980s. The Public Library Association does plan to have an Audio Producers Association panel discuss the basics of selection and handling in March 1994. Unfortunately, library scholars to date seem uninterested in audio books of any type.

Audio books' popularity is clear. Not only do most larger libraries and many small ones now have collections, but these collections are very well used. When I was working in the audiovisual department of the Durham County Public Library in the summer of 1987, I noticed that approximately 80 percent of the 85 titles in the complete audio book collection were in circulation at any given time. Now there are more than 1,000 titles in this collection, but according to Kathi Sippen, audiovisual librarian, 80 percent of these 1,000 titles are now continuously in circulation. The relatively affluent and highly educated citizens of Durham have insisted on a more than ten-fold increase in the collection, but the demand has grown apace.

In its guidelines for small and medium-sized public libraries, the American Library Association states that "Resources in any format, needed or requested by the library's public, should be considered for acquisition."[27] This, like all ALA policies, is a recommendation only. However it provides a clear framework for including the audio books medium. In weighing whether the provision of audio books is a needed service, it may be worthwhile to consider that their use allows people with different learning styles to enjoy books that they might not otherwise experience. Some people prefer listening to reading. This is one of the growth areas that could be important in drawing new patrons to the public library.

In addition to those individuals who merely prefer the sound experience, there are also people who suffer from a kind of cognitive dissonance in which their reading levels do not nearly match their intellectual levels. Included in this group would be those in reading classes, for whom the audio book has proven to be a helpful tool, at least in the school setting.[28] Recent immigrants who are learning or improving their English should also be considered. Laubach, the well-known publisher of literacy materials, now offers audio books especially written and recorded for new readers. They have a fairly high interest level and very simple vocabulary and syntax.

Another group that needs better access to audio books is the visually impaired. It is obvious that the Library of Congress Talking Books Program does not reach all those who are eligible for it, much less all those who might benefit. The U.S. Census estimates that 8,081,000 persons are suffering from visual impairments, but the Library of Congress estimates that only about 750,000 are receiving Talking Books on cassette.

Beyond these special cases are the mass of people who are capable of and enjoy reading but who prefer to listen for a number of possible reasons, including restrictive travel and home schedules. Time spent commuting, exercising, or caring for children is often available for listening to books but not for reading them. Also, eye fatigue caused by increased use of video display terminals as well as by reading print is probably on the increase. Many sufferers from insomnia find that, if audio books are not the cure to this disorder, they are an extremely benign treatment.

Besides these obvious benefits there are other possibilities. People will listen to books, authors, and genres that they would never choose to read. It is conceivable that people who listen to a audio book by an author whom they might not otherwise read or concerning a subject about which their interest is slight may become interested in this author or subject and make use of print resources. People may be drawn into the library who might not otherwise be there, and while there may be inspired to make use of more traditional services.

There have been some negative reactions to the inclusion of this medium in public libraries, but they seem not to have taken into consideration the ubiquity of the cassette player in this country. It has also been claimed that the abridged format is more practical than the complete, but this question will be dealt with in detail in chapter 2.

An objection concerning the importance of audio books is that relatively little important contemporary fiction is available in the format. I would argue that this is so not because the experienced listener can't understand and appreciate modern fiction, but because the market for these works is presently too small to justify first-class recordings. Recorded Books and Books on Tape already have recorded a number of prestigious titles, and Dual Dolphin offers still more from the British publisher Isis.

In many cases the fact that this medium is technically similar to video tape has led to confusion about the relative merits and roles of the two media. Until fairly recently, relatively few titles have been available and information about producers and distributors has been lacking. However, there are now tens of thousands of titles in many different genres, and this book addresses the information problem. Finally, isn't this medium just another way of facilitating the public library's most traditional service, books for people?

SOURCES

With the maturation of what can be described as a new art form, libraries have found themselves with an audiovisual service much closer to their traditional mission than videotapes, one that is otherwise available only to the affluent. Because audio books are expensive to buy or rent, libraries are finding them to be a popular service, though one which is sometimes difficult to manage. Little information is available on audio books, and acquisitions librarians often find themselves ordering very expensive materials almost in the dark.

The various sources for audio books can be divided into four groups. First are the producer/distributors (typically small corporations) who make and sell their own tapes. Books in Motion, Recorded Books, and Brilliance are examples of producer/distributors owned by entrepreneurs who set the policies and tone for the productions. The quality of these productions tends to be fairly consistent because the artists are given quite a bit of guidance by integrated production teams.

The second group consists of companies also usually owned and run by an individual but producing relatively few titles, their main business being buying rights and selling preexisting recordings. Typically their back list is very broad, including multivoice dramatizations, radio plays, and even (in the case of Mind's Eye) sound tracks of video productions. Books on Tape, the oldest audio book producer, is an example of a group-two producer/distributor, as some of their best titles have been produced by subcontractors like Joss Recordings and Ariel Productions. Other companies in this group include Listening Library and Blackstone Audio. The quality of these offerings may vary wildly, from Mind's Eye's great old BBC *Goon Shows* to mediocre unvoiced versions of out-of-copyright classics.

The third group includes both publishers that distribute audio book titles as a sideline, like Chivers, Nightingale-Conant, and Thorndike Press (Sterling Audio), and publishers that retain the rights to their own print versions and produce audio books, which can be excellent recordings. In the past these publishers have often been the only sources for British audio book titles.

In the future an increasing proportion of audio books, like the print versions, may be destined to be purchased through the fourth group, book jobbers. Ingram and Baker and Taylor have a long list of mostly abridged productions from the larger publishers, including simultaneous versions from the mainline book publishers. Ingram has also begun to distribute the Brilliance Corporation's complete versions at their standard discount of 46 percent, which makes these library editions highly affordable. Baker and Taylor also distribute Brilliance. There are now a number of jobbers who specialize in audio. Perhaps the best known is the Professional Media Service Corporation, which publishes the catalog *In the Groove*. The company has been in business since 1980 and offers competitive pricing and original cataloging (including MARC records). Competitors include Williamson, Bodner, and Audio-BookCassettes, who offer similar services and claim to be able to obtain any audio book. In my limited experience none of these claims should be relied upon with great confidence.

The audio books of groups one and two are often available through these jobber services. However, the real problems are pricing and replacements. Unlike book distributors, who offer considerable discounts, audio book suppliers tend to have prices as high as and sometimes higher than the actual publishers. What they are selling is convenience. A library that uses these services is trading personnel savings for extra expenditure on materials. It is possible to qualify for increased discounts by adopting standing order plans, but then the library gives up selection as well. Alternatively, some of the producers, most notably Recorded Books, will offer augmented discounts in return for standing orders and package deals. Obtaining replacements from services is another problem and often is slower and considerably more expensive than obtaining replacements directly from a producer. Again, the library is trading trouble and personnel expenditures for convenience.

FUTURE TECHNOLOGY

The future of books on cassette as an electronic format is also of interest to librarians now burdened with obsolete collections of phonograph records. There have been recordings of books on compact disk, most notably the HarperAudio version of Dylan Thomas's "Child's Christmas in Wales" and the productions of Spencer Library, Dove Audio, and the ZBS Foundation. However, opinions vary greatly among insiders. Behrens of Books in Motion "cannot imagine books on CD as a practical alternative. The technology is just not there."[29] Mike Comer of Sterling Audio on the other hand says, "Cassette tapes are a piece of technology headed for the boneyard. This is a lousy medium, you don't get good reproduction. In five years CD or some better medium will be demanded."[30]

A possible successor is Phillips Electronic's Digital Compact Cassette or DCC system, which was introduced in September of 1992. Its most important features are backwards compatibility, meaning that the machines will still play the older analog cassettes, and its sound, which comes close to that of a compact disc.[31] CD-Interactive and Sony Talking Type books are other innovations to be considered.

Most libraries continue to resist the idea of the electronic book. However, the audio book, which is one form of electronic access, is creating a bridgehead that cannot be ignored. Libraries seem to have no problem with electronic access for the librarians. The querulous comments concerning electronic access for library patrons remind me of a host of monks muttering in their beards about that upstart Gutenberg; they no doubt refused to believe that his crude techniques could ever replace the illuminated books of which they were so proud. To an extent, they were correct: The artistry of the illuminated manuscripts has never been matched—but they ceased to be produced just the same. No doubt the future of audio electronic access is as difficult to imagine as modern publishing was for the brethren. Yet librarians cannot avoid change by ignoring it and, in fact, may jeopardize the very existence of their institutions by doing so.

NOTES

1. Mark Annichiarico (1992), Playing for time: The delicate art of abridging audiobooks. *Library Journal, 117* (19), 41–44.

2. Mark Annichiarico (1992), Spoken word audio: The fastest growing library collection. *Library Journal, 116* (9), 36–38.

3. Dick Estelle (1990, May 30) [Letter to P. Hoffman].

4. Estelle letter.

5. Frank Muller (1991, July) [Interview with P. Hoffman].

6. Preston Hoffman (1992), Book Sounds. *Wilson Library Bulletin, 67* (1), p. 75.

7. Preston Hoffman (1992), Book Sounds. *Wilson Library Bulletin, 67* (3), p. 59.

8. Nathaniel Lande (1991), Toward the electronic book. *Publishers Weekly, 238* (42), p. 29.

9. Preston Hoffman (1992), Covert entry: The backdoor electronic revolution. *Wilson Library Bulletin, 67* (3), p. 36.

10. Lester Asheim (1987), *The Reader–Viewer–Listener.* Viewpoint Series, no. 18. (Washington, DC: Library of Congress Center for the Book), p. 16.

11. Asheim, *Reader–Viewer–Listener,* p. 17.

12. Asheim, *Reader–Viewer–Listener,* p. 19.

13. Preston Hoffman (1991), A change of voice: The art of the spoken word. *Library Journal, 116* (19), 41.

14. Muller interview.

15. Muller interview.

16. Hoffman, Change of voice, p. 41.

17. Sandra Burr (1991, August) [Interview with P. Hoffman].

18. Jane Sumner (1991, May 27), The voices that bring books to life. *The Dallas Morning News,* p. C1, C7.

19. Henry Trentman (1991, July) [Interview with P. Hoffman].

20. Hoffman, Change of voice, p. 42.

21. Muller interview.

22. Hoffman, Change of voice, p. 42.

23. Tim Behrens (1991, July) [Interview with P. Hoffman].

24. Toni Boyle (1991, August) [Interview with P. Hoffman].

25. Publishers Weekly (1991), *Audio Market Study Phase II—Among Libraries.* (New York: Cahners Publishing's Market Research Dept.), pp. 2–4.

26. Thomas H. Ballard (1986), *The failure of resource sharing in public libraries and alternative strategies for service* (Chicago: American Library Association), p. 140.

27. Audiovisual Committee, Public Library Association (1975), *Recommendations for audiovisual materials and services for small and medium-sized public libraries* (Chicago: American Library Association).

28. Barbara A. Bliss (1979), Help for unsuccessful readers: Recorded reading program gives pleasure and success. *Wisconsin Library Bulletin, 75,* 79–82.

29. Behrens interview.

30. Mike Comer (1991, July) [Interview with P. Hoffman].

31. Patrick M. Reilly (1991, July 11), The sounds of war: DCC vs. minidisc. *Wall Street Journal,* p. B1.

CHAPTER 2

The Relative Value of Complete and Abridged Audio Books

The controversy concerning abridged and unabridged audio books has been a significant issue among working librarians for a number of years. Although a growing number of library patrons and audiovisual librarians has become dissatisfied with abridged books, the price and other factors keep them in libraries, often as the dominant form. We will attempt to gauge the merits of the two formats in order to assist librarians to make well-informed policies and decisions.

The question of the relative merits and uses of complete and abridged audio books is at the heart of the selection and development of audio collections. I feel strongly that complete books are the wave of the future. As mentioned in chapter 1, a *Publishers Weekly* survey states that 90 percent of public libraries have audio tapes and 84 percent have spoken word fiction and nonfiction in their collections.[1] In public libraries, on average, 35 percent of the audio book collection consisted of complete books and 65 percent of abridged versions. Twenty-one percent of these libraries expect that these proportions will change in the coming year, with complete audio books increasing to 44 percent.

Given these figures, I will attempt to provide a balanced analysis by examining the views of some advocates of the abridged format. Unfortunately terminology obfuscates the issues, because it is so inexact as to be sometimes meaningless and always confusing. It may be a symptom of the low regard in which audio has been held that the commonly used term *unabridged* is a negative one. We assume that a codex is unabridged unless otherwise noted. In fact, the term *unabridged book* is redundant. Some may think that the issue of terminology is not important. However, literary theory and political science tell us that control of the naming function is tantamount to control of meaning and therefore of action. As Lester Asheim has written, "People base their expectation about a medium upon a few sample messages it may have carried, and as a result of that limited experience do not—or cannot—or will not—accept any other messages it is capable of transmitting."[2] I would add this is true not only about messages transmitted by a given medium but also about media.

The term *unabridged* has contributed to the marginalization of audio books service in libraries. Imagine, if you will, going into a library and finding that all books were abridged. You inquire of the librarian and receive a reply like this. "It's much more cost efficient for us to buy abridged books. Most of our patrons prefer them. We can add more titles with the same amount of money. The bookstores offer only these versions, and why should we be different?" Absurd as this sounds when applied to books, why should these arguments have any validity when applied to audio books? The negative terminology makes it easier.

This terminology has become standard for reasons having to do with economics and advertising. When the large publishers began issuing audio books in the 1970s through their subsidiaries, they did not wish to call attention to the fact that their versions were almost always less than the complete work. They attempted to make the abridged version the standard one. The words "abridged" or "condensed" appear in very small print in advertisements, catalogs, or on the works themselves—and in some cases not at all.

When complete versions finally began to reach the public, the small vendors of this product wanted to emphasize the difference in format. As their customers were often paying a quite high rental fee, often as large as the purchase price of an abridged audio, producers took their cue from the large publishers and defined their product negatively.

These reasons do not justify the uncritical acceptance of unabridged as the standard term. This is a young format that is just beginning to define its standards and for which the terminology is still in flux. I suggest *complete audio book* as a term that is fairer, more accurate, and more pleasing to the eye, tongue, and ear. Therefore we will use it as our standard expression throughout this work. Eventually the time will come when an audio book is considered complete and unabridged unless noted otherwise.

A symptom of the problems caused by the confusion of terminologies is the growing tendency not to label abridgments at all. One example of this is the Simon and Schuster version of *The Autobiography of Malcolm X*. In this case the audio book has bridges, read by an actor other than the main narrator, that connect selections from the book. A sophisticated listener, especially one familiar with the work, may or may not identify this as an abridgment. (Incidentally this is the first audio book to have received a highly publicized signing party in a Manhattan bookstore, Brentano's on Fifth Avenue. The primary reader, Joe Morton, signed the audio books.)

Another example is Penguin-Highbridge's audio of Salman Rushdie's *Haroun and the Sea of Stories*, read by the author, which had no indication on the package or in the catalog that it was in any way different from the original print version. It was only about three hours long, but this is a short book and the reading by the author is very fast. In fact, it was so fast that I got a copy of the book and sat down with the print and audio versions to see if I could follow it better with both. Only then did I find that the book had been rewritten. A check with *Words on Cassette* confirmed that this is an abridgment.

A good case can be made for abridging a work like Rushdie's. Storytellers say that they can convey information with their voices that must be put in words only for a written version. Donald Davis, perhaps the most outstanding storyteller in America today, is a purist about the distinction between telling and writing. "What happens when you write is you have to compensate for the loss of two thirds of the story, your body language and voice. What that means is that if someone memorizes that story and tries to tell it, it is going to be boring because there is way too much there."[3]

Penguin-Highbridge's *Haroun* may have been rewritten by Rushdie, in which case this recording would actually be another work by the same author with the same title. A label of "abridged by the author" or "a new version by Salman Rushdie" would have clarified the origin of the work in that case. However, we are not informed by the publisher who the abridger or editor may have been. We are left with confusion and misrepresentation. The identity of the individuals who do most abridgments is a tightly guarded secret. I have never seen or spoken with a practicing human abridger, nor are they generally identified. Usually their supervisors (sometimes ex-abridgers who have graduated to management) speak for them. Ghostwriters and romance authors are wild exhibitionists in comparison.

Then there is the question of the type of abridgment. Among abridgments there are wide variations. Some abridged versions contain only words that appear in the print edition, though in some cases more-or-less clearly delineated bridges connect sections. Others might be termed condensed, as they aim only at the general sense of the original. As Toni Boyle of Audio Book Contractors says, "The book is actually rewritten. I've done this myself many times."[4] As publishers generally do not distinguish among types, only a close listen with the book in hand will tell. Then there is the multivoiced reading, which may be complete except for the author's identifying tags.

There are valid justifications for the inclusion of audio versions of less than complete works in libraries, whether they are labeled abridged, condensed, excerpted, or diffracted, or even "audio scripts." Some libraries may continue to acquire abridged renderings as the main element of a collection. Is this wise, or should they be considered a transition format? Only the preponderance of evidence and the unique conditions of a given library can answer this question.

These renderings often are well done and may be the only ones available of a given title. This is especially true of nonfiction, much of which is not at this time being recorded in a complete version. Also, nonfiction recordings do not require the artistic and creative expertise of fiction. These recordings, often read by their authors, do benefit from the technical expertise available in the major publishers' studios.

Certainly the visibility and popularity of abridged audio has been helpful in bringing all audio into library collections. Abridged audio has established a high profile for audio books that complete audio alone might never have attained on its own. Abridgments continue to dominate sales in bookstores. Of the twenty audio books on *Publishers Weekly*'s Audio Bestsellers list as of January 1, 1993, nineteen are abridgments.[5] Most libraries began their spoken-work collections with either abridged or short-form versions (short stories, drama, poetry, etc.).

Another argument for the inclusion of abridged works is the demand for abridged audio from patrons. According to the *Publishers Weekly* survey, though 40 percent of libraries said their patrons preferred complete works, 21 percent said patrons prefer abridgments and 20 percent claimed no preference.[6] They see these abridged works in bookstores, often released simultaneously with the best-selling texts. On the other hand, although demand may be driven by advertising, it is questionable whether that is a valid reason for libraries to establish collections dominated by best-selling abridged audio. Especially in works of this type, as long as listeners can get the plot and an idea of the main characters they feel they have experienced the book and can hold their own in conversation about it. Even Michael Viner, president of Dove Audio and an ex-abridger, says, "[Patrons] may not lose much quality in their lives if they hear Judith Krantz's latest book in three hours instead of ten."[7] Like the best-selling texts, the audio versions are ephemera that will circulate strongly for a short time. Harper Audio's Maureen O'Neal is willing to say, "In many cases . . . a lot of books benefit from abridging, especially the thrillers, mysteries, and action-based novels."[8]

Paradoxically, the weaker the prose of a given book is, the better the abridgment usually is in relation to it. The standard audio book length of three hours reduces the average best-seller by about 75 percent. As this leaves time only for the plot, the main characters, and perhaps some action and sex scenes, the book may be considerably improved by the removal of verbal filler. This is a telling argument for libraries that intend to build collections of best-sellers.

Another popular argument is that the abridged book is a different form deserving consideration because it provides diversity in and of itself. Typical are the points provided by Mind's Eye representative Bob Lewis. He says, "A film is a different version of a book without being inferior, right? And the *Hitchhiker's Guide* was in audio before it was a book."[9] His company offers a great variety of titles from different producers, and he says, "I've listened to them all. We cherrypick; listen to everything and pick the best." A similar argument is made by Seth Gershel, vice president of Simon & Schuster Audio. "Audio is not supposed to be the book spoken: it's a different medium. It is not meant to replace the book or to be a read-along. The audio script is tantamount to a movie script."[10]

Some of these grounds are very good ones. For example, no one could criticize Donald Davis's audio versions of his originally oral stories, honed by repeated telling, for having fewer words than the print versions. Nor would it seem fair to require them to be labeled "abridged," as they represent the original versions of the stories. For the same reasons, if the audio version of *The Hitchhiker's Guide to the Galaxy* is different from the print version, it also seems beyond reproach. However the film-audio analogy seems spurious. After all, a book cannot be translated literally word by word to film, as it can to audio.

It is true that abridged versions have some elements added to them. Music and sound-effects plus a breakneck pace may help make some books palatable. Also, some listeners may have difficulty in listening to a complete and unadorned audio book. Going back and renewing familiarity with plot and relationships can be quite difficult with audio books. Defenders of abridged audio like Sherry Huber of Random Audio have a point when they call attention to certain basic differences. She says, "When you read a book, you can pick out parts that you might want to read again or skip over, because the book's format works wonderfully that way. But a performance does not necessarily work as well at great length. When you're listening to a story it's difficult to hold all the pieces in your mind, particularly if it goes on and on."[11] In my experience, listeners soon learn to retain the main characters and plot points in order to make the book comprehensible, if the book is good enough to make the effort worthwhile.

The cost of complete audio has long been an effective argument in favor of the abridged format. Certainly libraries can add many more titles by buying abridged works for the current industry standard price of $16 for two cassettes than by buying unabridged titles, which may cost more than $100 apiece. In fact, as distributors offer discounts of up to 45 percent, the savings seem tremendous. But these savings are a short-term gain at the cost of wise collection development. Would administrators fill their shelves with print abridgments of best-selling and classic works if these were available at an equivalent low cost? Would they ignore the patron complaints that would result from such a policy? Per cassette, even the most expensive complete versions are no more costly than abridged ones (before discounts that make comparison difficult), and works from the smaller producers are often cheaper.

Difficulty in obtaining complete audio also is a valid argument in favor of abridged versions. Most of the popular abridged titles are available at large discount from Ingram and Baker and Taylor, while relatively few complete versions are. This situation has been rapidly changing, however, as Brilliance now makes library editions available from Ingram at the standard discount. We hope that this book and others to follow will make the medium more comprehensible and easily managed.

For those who are celebrity-struck, well-known actors are common among readers of abridged audio but virtually nonexistent among complete audio books produced in this country (though some very well-known actors have done complete audio in Britain). It seems obvious that the quality of the reading should be more important than the identity of the reader, at least for libraries. In fact, *Publishers Weekly* found that though 55 percent of librarians thought well-known readers are important to some degree to patrons, quality of production was their most important selection criteria.

As authors have long excerpted portions of their work for reading in private as well as in public, ample precedent exists for the popularity of authorial readings. The question of authorial approval and authorial abridgments sometimes converge but often are widely divergent. The copyright laws require that an author or a representative approve any recording of a copyrighted work, but only in the legal sense. The major publishers ask us to believe that the authors actually read the scripts and pass on suggestions. Possibly this does happen in some cases, and no doubt it will happen more frequently. More likely, authors who care about the artistic integrity of their works will forbid abridgment, as do Jean Auel, Stephen King, Larry McMurtry, Sharon McCrumb, Amy Tan, and others.

It seems unlikely that many popular authors will spend time abridging their own work. There is perhaps a middle ground occupied by John Le Carre and Louise Erdrich. These authors have read their abridged versions very well. However, they were able to escape from the three-hour procrustean bed and produce abridgments that reduced their books by about half. *The Crown of Columbus* by Erdrich and Michael Dorris was read and abridged by its authors. A case can be made that this audio book is an example of another book by the same authors with the same title. However, it doesn't sound like a complete book. During the second half of the audio book, mystery characters and other anomolies make it clear this is a less than perfect abridgment. One similar variation is the repackaging of Le Carre's *The Secret Pilgrim*, which has been edited and reformatted into three audio books, not exactly abridged but different from the printed versions.

It seems likely to me that we will see more of these longer abridgments as well as more authors who cease to regard audio abridgments as harmless moneymakers somewhat like book club sales and begin to take the audio versions more seriously. I am told that it has become much more difficult to obtain reading rights for complete versions of quality best-sellers in the last few years. Speculation is that the large publishers are eventually going to produce complete versions of these books themselves.

Some books that are not necessarily ephemera may lend themselves to abridgment, or an abridgment can be a literary document in its own right. An example of this is the abridged version of Jack Kerouac's *Dharma Bums*. The reading by Allen Ginsberg, the original of one of the book's characters, makes the abridgment valid. This validation is a function not only of Ginsberg's celebrity but also of his not inconsiderable oral skills. On the other hand, the abridgments of classic works I have listened to tend to be absolutely incomprehensible. A reduction of *Pride and Prejudice* to the main plot points and the characters of Elizabeth and Darcy leaves a book similar to a Gothic romance but with incomprehensible structure and syntax.

There is a feeling of accomplishment that comes from reading a difficult classic that is diminished but not entirely destroyed by listening instead. Listening to an abridgment completely negates this feeling. Besides, who really wants a completely rewritten version of even a moderately skillful work?

Many abridgments are listened to by commuters who spend two to three hours driving per day, about one book's worth, though often the time listed on a package is exaggerated, as most run not three but two or two-and-a-half hours.[12] However, finding a new book of interest every day is not necessarily a desirable situation. This need can also be used to defend complete versions. For some, listening to a book is an exercise in filling fairly large blocks of time. There is no reason for them to rush to the end. Many of the occasional listeners I get will choose a book that will last about as long as the trip they are planning. This is much easier to do with complete works as well as more satisfying than choosing a number of abridged titles.

Music and sound effects are not necessarily detrimental to the quality of a presentation. The first-class productions of Spencer Library and the ZBS Foundation make this clear. Spencer's version of *The Fall of the House of Usher* with its original electronic score makes this book eminently listenable. It would be difficult for the most skillful reader to make the work nearly as interesting because most adults have far outgrown the jejune literary effects that Poe employed, if only because they have been extensively imitated and vulgarized. On the other hand, the music used in many of the abridged audios that I am familiar with consists mostly of canned strings and/or synthesized sound that appears mainly at the beginning or end of a side or to signal overwhelming emotion that neither the writer nor the reader is capable of conveying with word or voice.

The situation concerning sound effects is not dissimilar. Perhaps it is not fair to compare the assembly-line products of the major audio publishers with the works of Spencer or ZBS, both of whom use state-of-the-art technology to fool the ear and stimulate the imagination. However, the primitive but effective efforts of the old radio masters would seem to be fair competition. None of the sound effects on the abridged tapes can or in fact even attempts to reach this level. This kind of care and artistry would not be cost-effective. The situation is similar to that of animation in which computer-assisted graphics fall far short of the artist-intensive works shown in movie houses a generation ago. Abridged audio books have even less claim to craftsmanship than videos do. These versions will be forgotten after a shelf life only slightly longer than an avocado's, while even a weak cartoon will live on forever on cable TV.

Most importantly, abridgments are essentially ephemera. Replacement cassettes are rarely available and would not be economical at any rate, as processing costs would be greater than any savings. Complete audios, on the other hand, should last essentially forever. Every cassette in a given title can be replaced and replaced again at a cost similar to or even less than that of the original cassettes. Most producers offer a reasonable warranty period, and a number will replace at no charge worn-out or lost cassettes into perpetuity. The best titles will circulate almost constantly as long as libraries have the will to keep them on the shelves or until the present technology is obsolete. Even the equivalent print versions will be worn out and discarded and replaced repeatedly while an audio book continues to please numerous patrons.

In fact, library choice of format is a matter of attitude towards the medium and perceptions of use. It is perhaps significant that defenders of abridged audio rarely are able to cite specific titles as exceptional. (For the exception that proves the rule see *Library Journal*'s core collection of May 15, 1992.) If audio is to be treated as ephemera, a medium capable only of entertainment on the level of contemporary romance novels, then the abridged form is ideal. But if audio is considered equal in status to print materials, then libraries will want the complete versions. Libraries adopting the audio book as an integral part of their collections will naturally tend to emphasize complete versions. Those who believe the transfer of information is undergoing a paradigmatic change may want to consider the question carefully. Those who consider this a fad format that will fade as did the phonograph record and painting collections will do well to avoid cataloging their abridged materials.

NOTES

1. Publishers Weekly, (1991), *Audio Market Study Phase II—Among Libraries.* (New York: Cahners Publishing's Market Research Dept.), pp. 2–4.

2. Lester Asheim (1987), *The Reader–Viewer–Listener.* Viewpoint Series, no. 18 (Washington, DC: Library of Congress Center for the Book), p. 18.

3. Donald Davis (1991, March) [Interview with P. Hoffman].

4. Toni Boyle (1991, August) [Interview with P. Hoffman].

5. Audio bestsellers, January 1993 (1993), *Publishers Weekly, 240* (1), 31.

6. Publishers Weekly, *Audio Market Study,* pp. 2–4.

7. Mark Annichiarico (1992), Playing for time: The delicate art of abridging audiobooks. *Library Journal, 117* (19), 44.

8. Annichiarico, Playing for time, p. 44.

9. Robert Lewis (1991, July) [Interview with P. Hoffman].

10. Mark Annichiarico (1992), Spoken word audio: The fastest growing library collection. *Library Journal, 116* (9), 36.

11. Annichiarico, Playing for time, p. 42.

12. Annichiarico, Playing for time, p. 43.

CHAPTER 3

Selection of Spoken Word Audio

KATHI SIPPEN

Spoken word audio cassettes, especially in the form of audio books, open library doors to segments of the population who in the past seldom were users of library services. Others who have long been users of print materials now find the library playing a more important role in meeting their educational, informational, and recreational needs. Near-universal use of audio cassettes for recorded music has brought the cost of tapes and cassette players to a level that offers a potential market for an audio book edition of almost any marketable book. The durability, portability, and cost of this medium require that it be seriously considered for inclusion in every library's collection.

RATIONALE FOR BUILDING A COLLECTION

Establishing and building audio book collections in school and public libraries is important for many reasons. Among those reasons is compliance with the Americans with Disabilities Act. This legislation requires that libraries provide special materials for disabled individuals and make other materials readily accessible. An examination of patron types served by an institution will identify the immediate need. For instance, a school library providing services to visually impaired students should include audio books in its collection.

Libraries that serve students with learning disabilities can provide opportunities to listen to books and thereby achieve many of the same goals accomplished by students who read. Patrons with or without special needs can benefit from the inclusion of audio books in the collection. People who are not motivated to read may be more open to listening to books because of the added value of performance.

Research done in the Hosholm Public Library in Denmark is also relevant to the question of the educational value of audio books.[1] Interviews with children and parents found that audio books (1) did not decrease parental reading to children, (2) encouraged use of print, (3) stimulated language use, and (4) provided intellectual and emotional pleasure. Though the report doesn't indicate that this study is free of the natural tendency of parents and children to put a good face upon a practice they have found useful and enjoyable, its findings are encouraging. (Other references to education research are given in chapter 4.) Points two, three, and four may be relevant to adult use as well. Certainly the author is convinced of their value as she says, "We must learn to accept talking books just as we have accepted other new materials which have come into libraries in recent years, and of course give them the same critical evaluation as other materials."[2]

Public libraries tend to have a much broader patron base than school libraries. A rationale for developing spoken-word collections in public libraries can be established by an examination of the population of the community. Libraries that serve communities with large numbers of senior citizens should provide audio books for their patrons. Audio books are excellent for homebound patrons, many of whom are visually impaired. One of the fastest-growing groups of audio book users is the commuter. People who do a great deal of driving typically enjoy less leisure time than do others. Libraries can attract new patrons in this category by providing audio books. An unpublished study by Nancy Sabbe, director of the Madison (South Dakota) Public Library, showed that 60 percent of their audio book patrons are truck drivers. The poll also showed that classics were the most popular category, followed by a tie between mysteries and Gothic romances. To a great extent, it seems that awareness of the availability of audio books, especially complete ones, is the key to a broad patron base, as with many library services.

At the Durham County Library in Durham, North Carolina, we find that commuters account for a larger proportion of our spoken-word cassette circulation than do any other group. Furthermore, commuters are some of our most vocal patrons and provide valuable feedback. Commuters can be passionate in their requests for audio books. Also we often hear accounts of how tiresome music cassettes, as well as broadcast radio, become on long trips. One patron asserted that she would die if she could not check out audio books for her trips, an exaggeration, but clear testimony to the need.

Spoken-word cassettes attract students who might not otherwise patronize the library. Students whose assignments include reading a

Shakespeare play come to us in large numbers because the spoken performance is more meaningful and enjoyable to them. Parents of preschool as well as school-age children check out audio books. Parents often find that these materials promote an interest in reading and are a great source of quiet entertainment. Public and school libraries serving large illiterate or marginally literate populations can promote reading by providing audio books. At the Durham County Library we have noticed that an increasing number of adults whose reading skills are marginal is seeking out audio books as a way to stay informed and be entertained.

People who work with their hands or whose jobs require little concentration are often users of audio books. Among our patrons are many people who listen to books at their places of employment, as well as others who spend large amounts of time at home cooking, knitting, or doing housework or other chores. The range of patron types is broad. An examination of the library's community is critical in determining selections for small collections.

Once a collection is established, word of mouth is a terrific advertising tool, requiring no time, labor, or money. In fact, the tendency of many of our users to proselytize among potential patrons presents us with a challenging task: We must balance selection of new materials between serving the interests of our existing user population and the interests of prospective patrons who may not yet be aware of the medium.

SELECTION POLICY

Selection policies serve two purposes. They assist selectors in making the best choices with the resources they have and they provide documentary evidence supporting the presence or absence of particular titles when there are complaints about the composition of the library's collection.

In developing a selection policy, libraries find many preexisting guidelines. A selection policy must support or coincide with the mission statement of the library. The mission statement of a school library usually differs from that of a public library in that its materials are primarily supplements to the curriculum. Public libraries typically place their emphasis on selecting materials for educational, informational, and recreational values.

Every selection policy should cover the following topics: First, the objectives of the collection must be clarified. How will the collection support the goals of the organization? What are the goals of the organization? Does the audio book collection have any special role in accomplishing those goals (such as in providing materials to the disabled or to the marginally literate)? Goals of a school library change as curriculum changes; shifts in school populations, new educational programs, and trends in educational theory and practice all influence the library's requirements. Public library audio book acquisitions are likewise influenced by very much the same factors that determine print material selection policy. In addition, as an increasingly broader array of materials has become available on audio tape in recent years, libraries must be alert to new opportunities to achieve their goals.

Second, the scope of the collection must be determined. Will it include works for all segments of the patron population? Will it include abridged as well as complete works? Will it include all genres or exclude some? Most libraries will attempt to serve all segments of their patron population with audio books. If building a new collection is subject to budget constraints, it may be wise to focus on serving only selected segments initially. Each library can determine the focus of the collection based on the population types it expects to serve. Abridged versions of some nonfiction works (e.g., commentary and business) may be suitable to begin a collection for public libraries. Many school libraries will want to exclude all abridged works, and most libraries will reject or limit abridged fiction. Old radio programs, relaxation tapes, and recordings of storytellers may be very popular in public library collections. However, some genres may not be justified in a school library and perhaps should not be acquired for a public library until the collection is very mature.

Third, the choice of individuals responsible for making the selections is part of the policy. Selection may be directed by a general selection committee, the collection development librarian, or the nonprint librarian. Any role of the library director, library board, or school principal should be documented in the policy.

Fourth, the various methods of selection should be decided upon. They may include review sources, previewing some or all titles, on-approval purchases, and standing orders. Legitimate review sources should be described and requirements for documentation set forward. Responsibility for previewing should be spelled out. Standing orders involve an arrangement with a publisher to send a variety of titles of the publisher's choosing. The library should have the option of sending back titles it does not want. Discounts are often provided to encourage standing orders.

Fifth, how the library handles damaged tapes and replacement of tapes or collection maintenance is an ongoing problem. How and when titles are weeded may be decided using the same criteria as for books: physical condition of title, use counts, or dated or ephemeral content.

Sixth is how gifts are handled. Gifts sometimes provide valuable additions to a collection, but the library must ensure that it has in place mechanisms to make the processing of gifts economical. It must be made clear that adherence to the library's selection policy is required.

Seventh, a policy statement on intellectual freedom or a statement addressing the library's support of a diversity of views is absolutely necessary. Audio books may be treated identically with print materials with respect to censorship issues. Issues involving limitations on circulation to minors have arisen in some libraries in conjunction with video tapes and music audio materials but have not yet come up with respect to audio books.

Eighth is the procedure for a withdrawal request. Patron demands regarding collection content can give rise to controversy. The procedure for handling such requests should be clearly articulated.

Ninth are concerns about how a purchase request is handled. Not only should there be a well-defined policy for handling acquisition suggestions from patrons, but provision should be made for informing patrons of how their suggestions are handled and what the final disposition of any suggestions may be. The following is a sample selection policy for a public library.

Sample Selection Policy

Spoken word audio cassettes are provided to meet the evolving educational, informational, and recreational needs of our diverse community. As we work to strengthen the collection, we strive to make its scope as broad as the interests in the community.

Audio cassette is the present format of choice for spoken word. It is expected that spoken word will be widely available in compact disc in the future. Until audio books are readily available in that format, the library will acquire audio cassettes. The largest collection of audio books is housed at the main branch. Smaller collections are housed at the largest branches. All titles are available through intralibrary loan.

The adult fiction audio cassette collection consists of classic and contemporary fiction. Every effort is made to select in all genres: contemporary fiction, suspense, mystery, science fiction, romance, Western, adventure, classic. Full-length, complete (unabridged) titles are preferred over abridgments and excerpts, solely on the basis of patron demand. Popular titles that are abridged are considered only when there is demand. Multiple copies are ordered only for very popular titles in order to be able to afford a greater number of titles. Selection criteria include content, technical quality, and performance of reader. The same criteria as stated above apply to children's titles. Every effort is made to select titles based on books as well as recordings of renowned storytellers, legends, folktales, and the like.

Adult nonfiction titles include abridged and complete works in a broad range of subject areas: business, psychology, drama, self-help, language instruction, radio programs, speeches, biography, humor, religion, poetry, social issues, and others. Multiple copies of works are acquired only for very popular titles. Selection criteria include content, subject demand, technical quality, and author recognition. Performance of reader is not as much of a factor in nonfiction as in fiction.

Selection responsibility for audio books is a duty of the audiovisual librarian. Branch librarians are welcome to suggest titles for their own collections. Replacement of works takes place if there is demand for the title and the budget allows. Individual tapes are replaced in a multitape work to extend the life of a title. Selection sources and review sources include the titles listed above, as well as catalogues and patron requests. Orders usually go directly to the producers. All ordering is handled by the Resources and Technical Services Department. Gifts are accepted. The Audiovisual Librarian determines the suitability to the collection. The gift is placed in the Friend's book sale if it is not added to the collection.

Titles are removed from the collection for the following reasons: (1) Titles are worn or damaged. Normally defective tapes for a popular title are replaced one at a time, thus ensuring an almost infinite life. However, if patron complaints about sound quality or malfunction of more than one tape lead us to believe that the whole set is worn out, then it may be discarded and replaced or, if it is not a very popular or timely title, discarded without replacement. (2) Titles that circulate infrequently might be weeded in order to make space for new titles. (3) Titles that are no longer timely.

Reconsideration of spoken word titles: Titles are not automatically removed upon request. Patrons requesting reconsideration of a title must complete a complaint form, obtainable at any circulation desk. Complaints will then be considered by a materials review committee composed of the Director, Assistant Director, Division Heads, and the Audiovisual Librarian. The decision of the committee will be promptly communicated by letter to the complainant. Should the complainant wish to appeal the decision, he or she may request a hearing with the Board of Library Trustees. The library endorses the American Library Association's Statement on Intellectual Freedom.

SELECTION OF AUDIO BOOKS

Selection of audio books and spoken-word cassettes involves the consideration of more factors than considered in the selection of print materials. In fact, the selection of a good audio book is much more difficult than selecting a codex. Any print copy of *Huckleberry Finn* will do for the young adult shelf, though one may choose the Library of America edition for the .800's. But many versions of this work are available on cassette, and the differences are amazing. In fact, this art is changing so much that even recordings by the better producers that are five or ten years old are often greatly inferior to those of the last few years. Unfortunately, as copyright dates are often not provided in the catalogues, one may have to guess at dates by using the catalog number or develop a relationship with someone at the producer who will give appropriate advice. But whatever recordings are best in any company's list, they are almost sure not to be the ones on sale.

In books and periodicals we look at content, we take into consideration the shelf appeal of an attractive cover, and we may give some weight to durability and size. Important additional values must be judged in a book recorded on cassette. We must also look at production qualities: sound quality, performance quality, dramatization versus straight reading, and the addition of sound effects and music. We must give more weight to various components of packaging than we typically do in dealing with print. The technical quality of a spoken word cassette is extremely important. For the listener, it can make the difference between a mediocre—or even unpleasant—experience and a very satisfying one. Technical defects and technical misjudgments on the part of cassette producers can result in effects on the listener's experience analogous to the effects of typographical errors, misplaced pages, unreadable typefaces, discolored paper, and the inclusion of tasteless or irrelevant illustrations on the reader's experience. Fortunately the technology of book production has reached a stage at which library purchasers of print materials seldom must deal with physical quality problems. The spoken-word tape industry is not in any respect so mature as book publishing, and it is important that school and public libraries do their part to encourage audio book producers to provide products of better and more uniform quality.

Sound Quality

Sound quality is an important distinguishing characteristic of audio books. When judging sound quality, look for a clear and distinct reader's voice. It should not sound distant, muffled, or otherwise hard to hear. It should not seem to echo. There should be no background noise unless it enhances the text. The reader's voice should not alternate between faded and distinct; it should be consistent. Audio books should not sound as though they were recorded in a garage or cavern. (This is hardly an overstatement: Some publishers employ readers who provide their own equipment and location to record materials that are sent to them through the mails. All audio book recording should be done in sound studios with both technical and aesthetic supervision, but often it is not.) As with recordings of music, the sound should be clear with no background hum or any other distracting noise. Simply put, the sound should be pure, distinct, and clear.

Reader Style

The reader's style is something to consider as well. Does the reader enhance the work or detract from it? Does the reader add feeling to the work and make it come alive? Is voice inflection used to keep the listener interested, or does the reader maintain an unvoiced monotone throughout? Is inflection over-used, distracting the listener from the content of the work? The better producers choose readers whose voices are appropriate to particular works, while others seem to match their stock of readers with their titles almost at random. Listeners will find it strange and unsettling to hear a very feminine voice reading an action-packed thriller whose author wrote with a male voice. Similarly, a gruff male voice reading *Madame Bovary* would seem incongruous. These are extreme examples, but they point out the importance of a good match of voice and material.

What excites listeners is hearing a reader bring a work to life. A patron once reported to me that she never understood Pat Conroy's *Prince of Tides* until she listened to the Recorded Books' version. She said the reader (Frank Muller) was so skilled that she not only understood the book, she thoroughly enjoyed it. A skilled narrator is good at differentiating voices of different characters, or voicing. In books containing large portions of dialogue narrated by one reader, it is important that the reader change voices to match the dialogue and maintain each voice consistently. However, the current emphasis upon fully voiced works has led some actors to attempt characterizations that are beyond their range. This can make for a very unpleasant listening experience, analogous to a badly cast dramatic performance. Unvoiced and partially voiced recordings can be perfectly adequate if the material is suitable and the reader brings other assets to the performance such as emotion and pacing.

Appropriate dramatic quality is important for spoken-word materials of every form—not just for fiction. If you have not listened to any business, self-improvement, or other nonfiction cassettes, you may be surprised at how much the impact of various titles is affected by the dramatic qualities employed by the reader. Regular users of audio books often request works read by certain narrators. This is a testimony to the significance of performance in book recording. Astute users readily distinguish between professional, well-trained narrators and those who are inexperienced or poorly coached. Some producers set standards for excellence by marketing works read by professionals. Other producers definitely do not. See the results of a public library survey on audio book materials and producers in chapter 5 for comments on quality.

Words on Cassette[3] is a valuable tool for finding audio books by narrator reference. This work indexes narrators and performers and includes all spoken-word recordings they have done. Some producer's catalogues also index readers as well as titles.

To sum up, when judging an audio book, look for the following: Does the reading sound static, or does it flow and enhance the text? Does the choice of the reader match the book? Is the reader's voice suited to the material? Libraries are quickly becoming the biggest purchasers of audio books. It is important that producers of this product be kept informed about the overall quality they are providing. Librarians have an important role in requiring companies to raise the standards of excellence in the spoken-word format.

Product Packaging

The physical packaging of audio books is extremely important in a library setting. The three things to be aware of are the sturdiness of the package, attractiveness of the cover, and information provided on the cover. The people who are responsible for the processing of materials in the library are very appreciative of sturdy packaging for spoken-word audio cassettes. Patrons can be hard on library materials, and audio books are among the most delicate that are commonly circulated. Patrons leave cassettes in hot cars, take them to the beach, allow young children to have access to them, and use them with defective and nonstandard equipment. Those of us who work with these materials are concerned with how they hold up under adverse treatment.

Sturdy packaging also influences budgets because cassettes in packages that do not wear well must be repackaged by the library in the interest of extending circulation life. The ideal is to have a package that lasts longer than the tape inside. At this time cassettes are not available in "library bindings," but the importance of libraries to the audio book industry should make it possible for us to insist that standard packaging meet our requirements. This is another respect in which librarians can serve the interests of this industry and all of its customers.

The audio book review journal *AudioFile* has established a useful classification for packaging. They divide it into three categories: bookpak, the library-ready plastic packages that everyone prefers; airpak, styrofoam cases covered with paper that are suitable for limited circulation; and repak, all the myriad cardboard and flimsy plastic packages that publishers provide, none of which is suitable for library circulation. There is no way properly to attach pockets and security devices to them, they don't protect the cassettes well, and they don't last. For the most part, only publishers who do audio as a sideline and/or sell most of their products at retail continue to use repak.

However, even the plastic packages vary wildly in quality of appearance, durability, and convenience. One sign of quality is the presence of hubs, which prevent cassettes from becoming loose while in storage or being transported. Also, look for sealed covers from which the inserts cannot be removed. Recorded Books, Books in Motion, and Blackstone Audio probably have the most durable covers, though all three suffer from drab design. Books on Tape packages, like their recordings, vary quite a bit in design, though they are all drab but sturdy. The covers of Chivers and Brilliance seem to hold up less well than others.

Tape Quality

Most important, the life of a cassette varies depending on the physical quality of the tape: There are varying grades of tape quality. It is difficult to distinguish among the grades by appearance, but a general rule holds that the tape in screwed-together cassettes is better. It is easier to repair problems when the case can be reassembled. There are varying grades of tape players as well. Many patrons do not regularly clean their tape heads, which significantly diminishes the life of all the tapes they use. Patrons are often unaware of the importance of maintaining their equipment. Though difficult to evaluate, a modest program of user education in this matter that offers stickers on materials, posters at the circulation desk, and handouts to new patrons is a service that may pay off in reduced replacement costs. Heat and cold contribute to normal deterioration of tapes. Sand and dust can cause immediate damage. Exposure to magnetic fields may render a tape unlistenable. The bottom line is that tapes are fragile. However, the better the quality to begin with, the longer the life of the tape, even under adverse conditions.

The Cover

Labeling is important as a marketing tool. A spoken-word tape with an attractive cover and necessary information plainly visible circulates more frequently than a plain package with no information other than title. Patrons look for the following: an attractive cover, something that catches the eye; synopsis or description of the work; information about the narrator; and total playing time.

The most important of the factors that determine patron appeal is the description of the work. In all categories of spoken-word cassettes, the most frequent questions raised are those best answered by providing a synopsis of the work's contents. When the publisher supplies the needed information, it is very much appreciated by library employees. Whenever the library replaces the package of an item, the synopsis should be affixed to the package; it is information the patrons will ask for. Labor saved in getting an item on the shelf the first time is worth paying for (and publishers should know that!). Labor spared in ensuring that needed information is provided to the patron on the package reduces the value of the item and increases the costs associated with answering inquiries about materials. Certain companies are making an effort to provide the kinds of packaging most suitable for libraries. Books On Tape prints the name of the library on the titles the library has purchased from them—one less piece of work we have to do.

Shipping

Another question that may become important is that of shipping. If audio books are ordered from standard library distributors, they arrive with the books, which is usually no problem. Other publishers, however, may send their products by delivery services, ground or air, or by the mails. Generally, the faster methods result in less inconvenience and less damage to the cassettes and packaging, but sometimes the costs are passed on directly or indirectly to the library.

STORAGE AND DISPLAY

Lack of space in the library and/or lack of suitable shelving can be deterrents to creating a collection of spoken-word audio cassettes. Although storage and display problems may be presented as arguments against developing a collection, the favorable attributes of audio books should not be dismissed. Such constraints may require budget adjustment or reexamination of priorities, but they do not bear on the merits of developing an audio book collection.

Standard book shelving is not ideal for displaying audio books, although it is certainly adequate. Shelving that is tilted at an angle and backed is ideal for audio books. Any type of backing, even a low back, is preferable to no backing. Backing prevents all sizes of audio books from falling behind the shelf or forward off the shelf. The major library supply companies all market some type of tilted and backed shelving.

Libraries can consider shelving their audio books next to print copies on the bookshelves. Such a policy can eliminate the need for new and/or additional shelving and serves to draw the attention of patrons who may not ordinarily visit the audiovisual desk. Libraries should also be aware that some companies offer the option of purchasing catalogue cards and even MARC records. One might look for this type of service from a company before making selections.

The spoken-word collection usually is weeded out through attrition. Abridged tapes wear out; as they cannot usually be replaced, they must be discarded. Most of the weeding of the fiction collection takes place in this way. Nonfiction is different in that some titles may lose their currency or timeliness. Items that treat social issues often are found to be of only transient interest. Such works are candidates for withdrawal whenever it is observed that their circulation has waned. Be aware that most producers will replace single cassettes from multivolume sets free or at a price equal to or less than the original. Companies that do not have reasonable replacement policies should not get our business. See the directory of audio book producers/distributors in chapter 7 for information on replacement policies.

TOOLS FOR SELECTION/ACQUISITION: REVIEW SOURCES

AudioFile is a highly recommended monthly publication founded in 1992, published and edited by Robin F. Whitten and devoted solely to spoken-word cassettes. The reviews focus not on book content—because of an assumption that the codex has already been reviewed elsewhere—but on performance of narrator, technical quality, price, and other considerations. Reviews are submitted by librarians and others interested in the medium. A disadvantage is that the reviewers' standards are largely unknown. At first, *AudioFile*'s reviewers seemed quite uncritical, but lately they and the publication seem to be gaining in confidence, and the reviews have become more valuable. Along with the reviews, there is usually a short essay or two, often by an outstanding reader or someone else in the industry. A special feature is Double Takes, by Preston Wilson, who listens to and rates multiple versions of one popular title.

The *Wilson Library Bulletin* includes a regular column reviewing spoken-word audio cassettes on a thematic basis. This column is written by Preston Hoffman, who is allowed a great deal of editorial freedom. The disadvantage of having only one reviewer is that the number of titles covered and the viewpoint are limited, but the advantage of consistent standards is important. The *Bulletin* is published monthly (except July and August).

KLIATT, formerly known as *KLIATT Young Adult Paperback Book Guide* and *Audiobook Review*, is published six times a year. Jean Palmer edits the most complete reviews available. Their reviewers tend to review the book as text and as audio, but as reviewers' space is ample, this additional information is helpful. The format and procedures are similar to those of *AudioFile*, except that as an established publication they may have more editorial objectivity.

In *Library Journal*, Mark Annichiarico edits a regular section of spoken-word cassette reviews. One issue each year (November 15) is devoted to nonprint materials, and another article on audio books (sometimes survey results) usually appears in the May 15 issue. This publication has established the format and procedures adopted by *AudioFile* and others. Unfortunately most of the reviews try to criticize the work as text and audio and, as space limitations are stringent, often become overly crowded. Because advertising, especially by major publishers, is very important to *LJ*, critical reviews and articles have in the past been edited in favor of the large producers, though this seems to be less of a problem now. The *Journal* is published weekly (except for Christmas holidays and summer, when it goes to a bimonthly schedule).

School Library Journal, published monthly, includes reviews of spoken-word cassettes, with an emphasis on titles of interest to children and young adults.

Parent's Choice, published quarterly by Parents' Choice Foundation, includes titles of interest to children.

Booklist, published biweekly, contains very brief reviews, which sometimes seem to have been written without listening to the complete book.

School Library Media Quarterly, published quarterly by the American Association of School Librarians, is for school media specialists and educators at all levels.

REFERENCE TOOLS

Words on Cassette, published annually by Bowker, offers the most complete listing of spoken-word audio cassettes available. Indexed by title, author, subject, and reader, it also lists producers along with addresses and phone numbers.

Info-Trac Extended Academic Version, a CD-ROM, allows selectors to search for audio book reviews by title, author, keyword, and reviewer. A complete citation is provided, with a grade that indicates the compiler's opinion of the review's rating. Potentially very useful, especially for the larger library.

Producer's catalogues are sometimes very helpful. The bigger producers, such as Books On Tape and Recorded Books, include subject, narrator, and author indexes and a list of the nationalities of the reviewers. Annotations are provided in most catalogues. Sometimes a quote from a review will be included along with the annotation. (Such quotes are sometimes from reviews of the print version, not from reviews of the audio edition.) Other producers offer limited information, providing only title, narrator, and annotation. Length of playing time and number of cassettes is sometimes left out. This information is essential, and it is generally better to purchase from producers that provide more complete information about their products.

Compiling shelf list and circulation statistics as a aid to selection can be time consuming. If the library already owns a print copy of a work, that cuts down on the work of the selector, especially if the selector is not familiar with the particular title. The audiovisual librarian can call up the circulation record of the print version in order to determine if interest is already present. The library that has an automated catalogue can also generate use statistics to see what genres are the most popular, as an important aid to selection. Contact with other librarians involved with nonprint collections provides invaluable help in making decisions regarding audio book selection. Audiovisual committees and sections of library associations provide means of reaching other librarians with similar selection requirements. Tap this source; it is an endless supply of useful information.

NOTES

1. Barbara Bliss (1979), Help for unsuccessful readers: Recorded reading program gives pleasure and success. *Wisconsin Library Bulletin, 75,* 79–82.

2. Bliss, Help for unsuccessful readers, pp. 79–82.

3. *Words on cassette: Combining Meckler's* Words on Tape *with Bowker's* On Cassette (1993). (New Providence, NJ: R. R. Bowker).

CHAPTER 4

Audio in Education: Schools and Literacy

CAROL H. OSTEYEE

INTRODUCTION

This chapter will discuss using audio technologies in educational settings. Audio books and other audio materials belong in classrooms at all levels of instruction, from elementary to adult literacy programs, because listening is a basic skill involved in language development. Karen Kearns argues that it is the most basic skill in "The forgotten medium—Are we too visually dependent?"[1]

Research on learning styles has shown that people have strong preferences for visual, aural, or tactile modalities in learning situations. If, as Rita and Kenneth Dunn report, "Thirty percent of the school-aged population appears to be auditory"[2] and prefers to receive information by hearing it, then curricula and teaching should take this into account. People who have strong auditory preferences can readily learn from lectures, or recorded materials. Auditory learners remember 75 percent of what they hear, which means that audio books could be a powerful tool for them. Visual or tactile learners usually need to improve their auditory skills.

Another reason for using audio books is their usefulness in meeting the goals of developmentally appropriate curricula and the ways they can be used in whole language and individualized approaches to reading and language arts. These approaches will be described.

Finally, audio technologies allow and encourage children to explore the wide range of children's literature, often read by the authors themselves or by professional narrators and sometimes with background effects and music. This is a stimulating experience that is not dependent on reading level and certainly will create interest in reading. Rickelman and Henk have said it well: "The activity solidifies children's concept of story, encourages the use of prediction strategies, expands receptive vocabularies, captures the imagination, and most importantly, promotes further literary involvement."[3] A teacher or librarian cannot hope for more.

We will begin with elementary education and proceed through adult literacy programs. Complete audio books are the primary focus, but other types of recorded materials are also mentioned as they relate either to the specific needs of student populations or to teacher goals such as increased listening skills and comprehension.

ELEMENTARY EDUCATION

The main business of elementary school is the teaching of reading, writing, and the basic elements of mathematics, for success in later grades depends and builds on these three. Approaches to teaching reading have been subject to many swings, from phonics to sight word, from programmed instruction to open classrooms, and the concept of whole language is currently being incorporated in many reading programs.

Whole language can be described as including all facets of communication (listening, reading, writing, speaking, viewing, and language arts skills) in ways that derive from and utilize "natural" English language literary forms. "A whole language classroom is literature-based, recognizing that trade books provide language models that are of high interest to children. Basic reading skills are addressed as children interact with the whole piece of literature."[4]

Another current educational effort is called the developmentally appropriate curriculum. Developmentally appropriate curricula for young children seek to provide active, participatory learning experiences (typically with centers where subject areas such as math and science are taught to small groups of students, who move from center to center), with many sensory inputs (i.e., hands-on activities and manipulatives). Children are not forced through levels of development or performance before they are ready. Rather, it is accepted that learning is continuous and accomplished at different rates by different children. Multi-graded classes and ungraded report cards (no number or letter grades) characterize these settings.

Developmentally appropriate classrooms in grades K-3 generally include a whole language approach, but it is also used in more traditional or transitional classroom settings, sometimes as part of centers devoted to reading, writing, listening or language areas.

Audio books can serve the purposes and methods of the whole language approach to reading, and many teachers could consider their use when principals and administrations ask them to change in such a direction. Interest in developmentally appropriate curricula has led to learning centers in many early childhood classrooms; a center devoted to listening is now commonplace in the lower elementary grades.

Though some teachers have always had listening centers (even when not educationally fashionable), they tended to be identified with enrichment activities; in many cases, this meant a reward for advanced students. Redbirds and Yellow Birds who never managed to finish first rarely made trips to those interesting corners of the room.

It is my position that because students are at different points in the learning-to-read process, K-6 classrooms should all incorporate listening areas or centers into daily instruction and offer it to all levels of students. This is one way to use whole language in teaching, to allow for individual development and to accommodate the different learning styles found in any group of students. We will look at some kinds of listening experiences and how children can be taught through them.

In center-based classrooms, it is easy to devote one center to audio experiences. Many teachers find that placing a reading corner (with print material) next to a listening area works well; the listening devices and material also may be made part of a reading area. Centers are usually managed so that children visit and/or master each center activity on some predetermined schedule, such as once a day or twice a week. Record-keeping systems keep children on task: for example, kindergartners may rotate to color-coded centers and accumulate stickers or colored clothes pins as they complete the center activity. Within the listening center, the activity may be a choice of audio books or a directed lesson, perhaps followed by a listening choice.

Readers, from first grade up, can use checklists at each center or work from a daily/weekly contract. The order in which students rotate to centers can range from a fixed schedule to completely open, but it is limited by number of chairs or a size limit. Here again, teachers may want to combine a directed-listening and free-choice activity so that students both share a common experience in literature and develop their own tastes by selecting listening materials. I recommend this because of the advantages to both student and teacher of including structure and decision-making, for example, "After listening to *Play Ball, Amelia Bedelia,* choose two other tapes and write their titles on your contract. Then write a paragraph about how these works are different from, or similar to, each other. Check yourself off when done."

Using schemes such as these with listening centers will ensure that all children get to listen to audio books as part of the daily routine. Selection or production of materials then becomes the teacher's biggest job.

More traditional classrooms, with desks for each child and more whole-group instruction, can still contain areas for listening and reading. Or a teacher may use whole-group listening to audio books, in particular shorter works (15–25 minutes). The peripheries of a classroom may be set up with tables for this purpose, as students are finishing work at different rates. Some suggestions follow about how listening to audio books and other materials can be part of a more structured approach.

1. Set up a listening table or area, with limits on the number of participants (because crowding disturbs others in the room and destroys the continuity necessary for successful listening). Have a specific number of chairs or pillows to match headphones. Three to four students per recorder seems to work well. Teachers and librarians must establish and discuss guidelines for the treatment of tapes and players, cleanup, cooperation, and so on. These should be posted in the listening area. Having guidelines is important because tapes, books, and equipment require care and respect. Labeling one set of headphones as LEADER eliminates arguments over who touches the cassette player and tape.

2. Audio book titles and authors are listed on charts and posted in the listening area. This step encourages planning and decision making and makes another connection with reading print. By announcing the available audio tapes, the teacher or librarian is showing their importance and even legitimacy (in the sense that things are "public") of listening to students. It also serves as a record of what has been put out and when.

3. Change audio books about every two or three weeks. Interest in selections will peak and then rapidly descend, though a few favorites may be returned to the collection periodically (a type of intermittent reinforcement). Changing selections regularly encourages their continued use, and occasional reappearances are appreciated.

4. Plan for times when students can use the listening center(s), but don't leave times unstated or vague. Some possibilities are:

a. As a choice when students finish work. This option should be posted in the room.

b. Before school officially begins.

c. During a snack break. Even ten minutes will be used for listening by some students, especially if they can eat a snack as they listen.

d. Instead of a regular lesson. For instance, a special education student could listen and read along silently, instead of taking a class spelling test that will not contribute to a grade anyway. Or a student who has mastered multiplication tables may listen instead of doing a review math lesson that most of the class really needs. This suggestion requires flexibility on the teacher's part.

e. During D.E.A.R. (Drop Everything And Read) or Silent Sustained Reading (SSR). A sign-up sheet for listening will help organize listening and let all students have a chance. Teachers who have individual classroom cassette players and headsets (such as Walkmans) can let students listen at their desks. During a 25–30 minute period, such as SSR, a student can become involved in longer works. This is a valuable time for listening and reading.

f. After school, if some students wait in the room for bus loading, car rides or after-school care.

5. Select a wide variety of materials for varying interest and reading levels. Selections should be word-for-word and complete. Students can be involved in the selection process after they are used to having a listening program with audio books ("Let's talk about the kinds of things you want to listen to. What have been your favorites during the last month? Why? What kinds of books would you like to have more of?").

My classroom assortment for third grade typically includes a classic or two, a popular trade book (Disney or Berenstain Bears, for example), some poetry ("A Rocket in My Pocket"), a class-made tape (students reading stories they have written), a nonfiction piece when available, and something musical, usually with the lyrics alongside. Whenever possible, provide the printed book so that students who want to read along with the tape have the option to do so. Listening and reading along simultaneously reinforces the experience because two communication modes are operating together within a meaningful context. I have found, however, that stress is reduced if students realize that they need not always follow along in a book.

Nonfiction audio tapes should also be provided for elementary, particularly teenage, students. Children like nonfiction, especially as they get older. Teachers, however, report that children's favorite choices for reading aloud are fiction; the effort to overcome this preference and to use and enjoy nonfiction must therefore come from us. We will be helped in finding nonfiction tapes by taking heed of the interests of our students or patrons. Whether teacher-read or played on cassette, nonfiction deserves a place in classrooms and libraries that is at least equal to that of fiction.

6. The Listening Library, Inc., has published *The Listening Road to Literacy,* a valuable collection of audio activities.[5] This guide includes 31 activities for grades K-3 and 30 for grades 4-6, which came from public school teachers who field-tested them, thanks to a grant from Listening Library. I found them to be practical and worthwhile for both teachers and school librarians to consider. All the audio activities are keyed as to whether they work best with individual children, small groups, or a whole class.

Most of the activities in this guide could be done in reading or language classes without the use of audio tapes, but this is another way of saying that a good teaching idea or technique can have many applications, depending on the audience and circumstances. One example of a 4–6 activity that is dependent upon audio books, which I found intriguing, appears on page 80. It is designated as whole group and could be called Guess My Title. (One criticism of this guide is that activities are only numbered, not named. I think teachers would appreciate having a title for any activity they are going to use and include in a planning book.) In Guess My Title, the class works in teams to come up with a book's title after listening to a brief excerpt (30 seconds) from a cassette. "Later, challenge the students to guess while allowing them to listen to shorter and shorter portions of the book." It was not explained whether students were familiar with the excerpted work or whether the goal was to listen "blind" and use their creativity and imaginations to come up with titles. Presumably, the activity could be used either way.

People just beginning to set up a listening program may benefit from the chapter entitled "Tips for Using Audios to Promote Literacy." Also of practical value is the last chapter, "Audio Cassette Repair" (or see this article as it appeared in *Library Journal,* November 15, 1989, by Doreen Bolnick and Bruce Johnson).

The Listening Road is recommended with the caveat that all audio titles are (naturally) from Listening Library. Activities for the upper elementary grades, 4–6, are not usually easy to find, which makes this publication all the more welcome. The address for Listening Library, Inc., appears in chapter 7.

A word about "Cliffhangers," which predominate in the guide's audio activities for grades 4–6. These are audio tapes that are narrated up to an exciting point in the story (often one-third of the way into the book) and stop there for students to finish reading on their own. I do not recommend cliffhangers for collections because they deprive teachers, librarians, and students of a full resource. Any complete recording can be turned into a cliffhanger, but not the reverse. Having a complete tape of a work is much more useful than a partial recording, especially for those students who will not be able to read the book to its conclusion. However, cliffhangers do cost less than complete audio books.

7. Plan materials so that special topics, themes, or authors (from areas such as social studies or science) are stressed. When topics from other subject areas are included or taught through listening activities, a teacher is integrating skills and learning across the curriculum. Integration of subject matter is a sensible goal in elementary education because students are likely to retain more and to have deeper understanding when learning is connected to several subjects and has a real-world basis.

8. Some literature-based reading series, such as those from D. C. Heath, come with good audio tapes. I have found that students eagerly listen to these when they are available in the listening area, but my preference is to wait until we have read a selection before playing it for the class or putting it out. In my experience, not only slow readers, but all readers enjoy listening to this literature from the basal text over and over. This is probably because literature-based basal readers contain much excellent material and because students who have read and listened to selections like to encounter them again and feel their mastery of the words and stories.

9. Teacher, librarian, or volunteer-made audio books are valuable too and will increase your resources immensely. Marie Carbo, in "Making books talk to children," has many suggestions for making audio books.[6] Her article tells "How to record storybooks in a way slow readers can follow, and set up a story center where they can listen and read." The beauty of making your own audio books is that the pacing can be adjusted for slow, insecure readers and nonnative English speakers. Commercially produced tapes model fluent speech and reading patterns, but may be entirely too fast for perhaps a third of most classes to follow.

Dr. Carbo has expanded the idea of taping books for at-risk younger readers in her 1989 book, which comes with an audiotape of samples.[7] She advises that very small amounts of text be recorded, on only one side of the tape. Children should listen repeatedly and read back passages that are above their reading level. Because of the slow pacing, this approach doesn't work with longer works unless one uses excerpts. *How to Record Books for Maximum Reading Gains* is a useful book for step-by-step information about recording books at or below the third-grade level.

Of course, there is room for both the homemade and the commercial. Teacher-made tapes can include questions following the story that students may answer orally or in writing; the possibilities are endless.

10. Children can also record books, either for their own grade level or for cross-grade teaching. For example, sixth graders can produce audio books for younger students and then receive critiques from their audience. This project takes the activity of children reading books aloud to each other one step further; ideally, every child in a room would be recording his or her own tapes throughout the year. Students should make up questions (and answers) about the selection and should follow through by being teachers and seeing how well their peers listen and comprehend.

11. Repeated Readings with Tape-Recorded Material (RRT, as described by Richard Conte and Rita Humphreys)[8] is a technique, similar to Carbo's, that can improve oral fluency in reading. In this remedial method, students first listen to a tape of a given passage, read along silently while tracking the words, read along orally with the audio, and then read unassisted—and repeatedly—until they are able to read the passage fluently. RRT is one example of how audio books from the listening corner can become instructional, and vice versa.

12. Lessons can be taught to improve listening. "Listening is a skill which requires a good deal of practice to perfect," says Karen Kearns.[9] She stresses the cost-effectiveness of using audio material as teaching tools, while admitting that teacher time and effort is required. The content can be literature or recordings from sources such as National Public Radio.

An activity that has been used with junior and senior high resource-room students is described by Patricia Forster and Beverly Doyle.[10] Their audio tapes contain current news items: "The teacher makes a tape recording of the morning news broadcast [and] then develops an outline frame, which includes background concepts and vocabulary." In their study, students improved both their listening skills and awareness of current events.

13. Specific language arts or reading lessons can be taught around audio books. For example, I played *Owl Moon* by Jane Yolan for third-grade students, who listened and followed the text in groups of three, sharing books. The story coordinated with animal study and the winter season in science and was used to reinforce a lesson on adjectives. Students summarized the story orally (reviewing this skill) and were directed to find ten describing words from the book. These words were used in other sentences that they made up. Other dimensions that we explored were the way students felt about the book and how the adjectives used throughout created these feelings.

14. Sometimes my class will listen to an audio book as they work independently on an art project. Ghost stories, short stories, and storytelling have worked best, and the mood has been conducive to creative expression. Students still whisper, which is permitted unless other classmates complain. Students need to talk about their art, but we reached a balance, and the audio tapes were enjoyed at these times.

15. I have encountered a problem with younger students, that of how to get them through works that take up two or more tapes. Even with flexible programming, this consumes a sizable part of a day. Spreading the work over several days runs the risk that the students will lose the story line or momentum. A possible solution might be having a supply of classroom tape players. For approximately $20 each, a teacher could distribute individual players and headsets so that students can pick up and continue a story when they have the time.

Another solution I have tried is to use the longer work as a read-aloud book over several days' time and, when the reading is completed, to put the audio book in the listening area for students to choose. This has worked because students maintain high interest in a live reader;

summarizing, questioning, and paraphrasing have helped students review previously read sections; and sometimes I have gone back over
several pages to help the students make sense of the story.

We have listened to longer tapes during classes that require repeti-
tive skills, such as cursive handwriting. While students practiced writing, they listened to *There's a Boy in the Girls' Bathroom* by Louis Sacher.
At twenty minutes twice a week, it takes a while to get through an
entire work, but student comprehension was good and they looked forward to the listening. The last five or ten minutes of the day have also
been devoted to listening to longer works.

MIDDLE OR JUNIOR HIGH SCHOOL EDUCATION

Middle or junior high school uses of audio can be extrapolated from
ideas in the elementary education section (applying them upward, as it
were) and secondary-college ideas (by adapting them down). The middle-school years have popularly been called "forgotten years," and I
have not located many resources that specifically apply to these grades.
I believe, anyway, that one can pick and apply any sound teaching idea
to any level, if one considers interest, maturation, and ability.

Betty Carter and Richard Abrahamson are definitely addressing the
needs and interests of adolescents in their article, "Nonfiction in a read-
aloud program."[11] They persuasively argue for teachers to read aloud
more to middle and high school classes, citing increases in motivation,
vocabulary and reading comprehension as benefits. Although teachers
report fiction as their favorite choices for reading aloud, nonfiction—
especially ghost stories, adventure, biography, historical narrative, and
humor—seem worthy of inclusion in both read-aloud and audio book
listening programs. Because class periods are limited in these grades
(to 45–50 minutes) and students shift from teacher to teacher, the use
of excerpts might be wise, with students doing independent reading or
listening at other times, perhaps as homework or study hall assignments.

"Teaching tips for using audio cassettes in literature classes" can be
found in Rose Reissman's pamphlet.[12] Dr. Reissman's thirteen-page
teacher's guide is published by Penguin USA (see chapter 7). It seems
applicable to both middle and high school grades. Her mission statement deserves consideration because it puts the use of audio books in
a broad framework: "Through the use of audio cassettes in literature
classes . . . students can use their own learning styles as a catalyst for
in-depth study of masterworks. With the broad implementation of
whole language literacy approaches, which encourage both the classroom teacher and the librarian to teach reading in a rich multisensory
environment, librarians justifiably include audio cassettes as part of

their 21st-century literacy mission. Collaboration by librarians and teachers in integrating audio cassette experiences into critical reading and writing instruction can measurably enhance these skills."

Five strategies for using audio tapes are proposed by Dr. Reissman, all of them employing excerpts (generally three to ten minutes of a work or two or three pages worth of writing). Using excerpts makes sense when teachers are squeezed into rigid time periods. Strategies are described in three parts: before, during, and after the playback. The five strategies are as follows.

1. Students will explore the elements of an audio production. This enables students to develop familiarity with terminology and concepts.

2. Students develop listening skills and practice listening. My one reservation is about having students make word-by-word transcriptions of what they hear. This activity might be tedious and frustrating for many students, and I fail to see how it would improve listening.

3. Students develop a prequel by listening to a carefully selected excerpt and writing and/or taping scenes that could precede it. This activity is completely dependent upon the choice of a workable excerpt.

4. Students compose storyboards to understand plot. Dr. Reissman states that this activity will appeal to visual learners and could be used in adult literacy; I agree.

5. Students transform the work from audio tape to a new genre, such as a visual art form. I found this to be the most interesting activity, one that calls for critical thinking and creativity.

These teaching strategies could be expanded and extended in many ways; for example, students could make their own versions of audio books. This publication is worth having at all educational levels.

One middle-school teacher reported that he planned six lessons around a particular work of literature. The lessons lasted for one or two weeks of classes. One lesson was a directed listening assignment, either on the work under study or a related work. Students rotated to all six lessons. This arrangement resembles a centers-approach for older students.

Sharon Briggs and Ginny Sorrell, two intermediate teachers in Fairfax County, Virginia, have tested and developed a recorded book program to help at-risk students. They call it a classroom content program because the taped material consists of the regular textbooks and novels that make up the curriculum. Volunteers tape the chapters, using an adaptation of the directed reading with questions technique (SQ3R, or Survey, Question, Read, Recite, Review). In their teaching of seventh graders, Briggs and Sorrell found improvement in reading fluency, grades, self-esteem, and leadership skills.

Some important aspects of this method are having tape players available in the classroom, circulating tapes overnight, and making students read along with the tape. Their readings are paced so that the smooth flow of the story is not interrupted. People who are interested in following Briggs and Sorrell's example can obtain a two-tape package, *How to Rescue At-Risk Students.*[13] Please note that Briggs and Sorrell took the following precautions because textbooks, workbooks, and consumables are not covered under fair-use copyright exemption for teaching situations: "We wrote the publishers of the books explaining the needs of our students and the taping program we were developing. We asked for permission to record their book so that non-fluent readers could read the content and listen to a fluent reader at the same time."[14]

Teachers in nonprofit educational institutions need not worry about taping or performing copyrighted material as long as these works are used in the course of face-to-face teaching activities. The *Copyright Handbook* further states that "the activities should be carried out by instructors or pupils in the classroom or similar place devoted to instruction."[15] Teachers may even make multiple copies of their own readings as long as they do not exceed the actual number of students in the class.

SECONDARY EDUCATION AND COLLEGE

In English and literature courses, teachers can use audio books in SSR as well as to serve instructional purposes, such as guided reading or listening after the class has read part of an assigned work. The classics and other nonfiction and fiction audio books typical of secondary education could naturally fit into instruction and encourage discussions of style, tone, and the like. Comparisons of different readings of the same work would be worthwhile, and this technique could be used in lower grades, too. At this level, the same selection criteria are possible as for regular adult and young adult listeners (see chapter 3) although teachers will also be working with a syllabus or set of curriculum guidelines.

Other recorded materials, such as National Public Radio tapes, could enhance the teaching of social studies, history, and economics. This is one way to bring the real world into the classroom and make learning relevant. In a college course on the teaching of reading, I used an NPR tape called "A Sound Portrait of Noam Chomsky" (from "A Question of Place" series). By playing this tape in sections, with pauses for outlining, clarification, and questions by students, we were able to hear about deep structure in language in a way that held student attention and brought us in touch with the genius behind the work. Doing so certainly took more effort from all of us, but we were able to increase understanding from the activity, and the lesson was structured so that students could interact with the ideas and with me.

Audio books can serve for remediation in secondary education as they do in the elementary grades. As in the technique of Forster and Doyle described previously, taped news items could be used to improve listening skills in remedial students and teach study skills to all students. The approach of Briggs and Sorrell would also apply.

Special kinds of audio tapes are valuable resources in terms of providing experiences that are beyond the scope of teachers and librarians. Chaucer comes to mind. Not many high school teachers are skilled in Middle or Old English, but tapes of Chaucer or Beowulf being read correctly can make these languages a living experience for students. Likewise, poets reading their work and played on tapes can open up the classroom or library to verse in ways beyond most teachers' ability. The same is true for tapes of Jack Prelutsky and others reading their poems for children.

One way to use recorded books, but not the whole work, is described by Marie Carbo as Storytell-Record-Storytell-Record.[16] By storytelling, she is referring to giving a summary of, say, the first three chapters of a work. Chapter 4 would then be recorded word for word, and students would listen to this chapter in class. The pattern repeats until the story ends. As an extension, students could provide summaries (after a homework reading assignment), either orally or in writing, and compare them with the taped summary.

ADULT LITERACY PROGRAMS

In recent years, a new breadth of programming has become available in adult literacy. The field itself has matured since Frank Laubach began the first organized system for teaching adults to read. Part of this maturation reflects awareness of adult new readers as a diverse group of people with different learning styles. Another change is taking place in the approach to instruction itself. "Rather than just teaching decoding skills, the emphasis is now on building on the learner's existing skills and integrating all types of communication skills."[17] Curricula are much more varied and interesting than the earlier phonics-only, programmed approach.

Laubach Literacy Action (the United States program of Laubach Literacy International) encourages the use of many innovative materials, including audio tapes. Their New Readers Press produces a variety of audio tapes that are of high interest but low vocabulary and reading level (see chapter 7 for an address).

Specifically for promoting family literacy are folk tales, fables, and Mother Goose rhymes, all at a second or third grade reading level. These can be purchased with read-along tapes for adult new readers to use with their own pre-reading and beginning-reading children. For pleasure reading, adults can choose short stories with themes and characters designed for them, again with read-along tapes. Adult new readers and tutors have reported informally that these tapes are popular and constantly circulated by organizations such as literacy councils.

Another series with tapes helps English as a Second Language students (first- or second-grade reading level) deal with adjustment themes or belonging to a new culture. A fiction collection (22 titles) of study packs (books and tapes) has a third-grade reading level and offers teacher's guides to assist tutors or instructors. A few books with tapes are written at the fourth-grade level.

Even if audio books are not used for tutoring or instruction, they can be used as with regular adult and young adult listeners—for exposure to literature, to increase fluency of vocabulary and language patterns, to lead into more guided and structured activities, and of course for pleasure, to foster a love of reading.

CONCLUSION

This chapter has advocated the use of audio books and other audio materials as part of daily teaching and in public and school libraries. Many possible ways to use audio books have been presented. Implicit in this point of view is a new relationship between teachers, media specialists, and librarians in schools and public libraries. Teachers and librarians will need to communicate more as they seek, together, the literary experiences they want to provide to students. A higher level of cooperation will be necessary because literature (in print and audio) will be moving between library and classroom in more complex and faster-changing patterns. Susan Prillaman is referring to a new role for librarians (in predominantly whole language schools) when she writes: "Teachers alone cannot be expected to be aware of all the currently available learning resources, as well as what are emerging resources and technologies. Teachers can come to rely on the media specialist to locate, acquire, organize, and teach teachers how to use them."[18]

Other reasons for using audio books have been proposed here. At a basic level, audio books give students and library patrons more experiences in listening and literature. This is one way to help people love reading in general. Moreover, people who learn best by listening and who are not good visual learners will feel comfortable and appreciated if audio materials are included in instruction or on library shelves. The recent trend is toward accommodating learning styles and preferences in classrooms and libraries.

Teachers can begin to use a whole language approach through audio books. A balanced use of basal readers, whole language, and instruction in language skills seems a wise way to avoid the effects of drastic swings in educational philosophy. A positive attitude towards listening to audio books will encourage the people around us to listen. The ideas presented here will not all appeal to teachers or librarians, but they may help you get started.

NOTES

1. Karen Kearns (1985), The forgotten medium—Are we too visually dependent?" *NASSP Bulletin, 69* (480), 45–49.

2. Rita Dunn and Kenneth Dunn (1993), *Teaching secondary students through their individual learning styles* (Boston, MA: Allyn & Bacon), p. 402.

3. Robert Rickelman and William Henk (1990), Children's literature and audio/visual technologies. *The Reading Teacher, 43,* 682.

4. Karen Bauer and Rosa Drew (1991), *Lesson plan book for the whole language and literature-based classroom* (Cypress, CA: Creative Teaching Press), 4.

5. Marshall Thurber (Ed.) (1990), *The listening road to literacy* (Old Greenwich, CT: Listening Library, Inc.).

6. Marie Carbo (1981), Making books talk to children. *The Reading Teacher, 35,* 186–189.

7. Marie Carbo (1989), *How to record books for maximum reading gains* (Roslyn Heights, NY: National Reading Styles Institute, Inc.).

8. Richard Conte and Rita Humphreys (1989), Repeated readings using audiotaped material enhances oral reading in children with reading difficulties. *Journal of Communication Disorders, 22,* 65–79.

9. Kearns, Forgotten medium, p. 49.

10. Patricia Forster and Beverly Doyle (1989), Teaching listening skills to students with attention deficit disorders. *Teaching Exceptional Children, 21* (2), 20–22.

11. Betty Carter and Richard Abrahamson (1991), Nonfiction in a read-aloud program. *Journal of Reading, 34,* 638–642.

12. Rose Reissman (1992), *Teaching tips for using audio cassettes in literature classes* (NY: Penguin USA).

13. Sharon Briggs and Ginny Sorrell (1991), *How to rescue at-risk students,* 2nd ed. (Cassette Recording) (Clifton, VA: Sound Reading Associates).

14. Carbo, *How to record books,* p. 73.

15. Donald F. Johnston (1982), *Copyright handbook,* 2nd ed. (New York: R. R. Bowker Co.), p. 158.

16. Carbo, *How to record books,* p. 24.

17. Betsy Stubbs (Ed.) (1992, Summer), *Trainer Touchstone* newsletter (Syracuse, NY: Laubach Literacy Action), *9,* 1–8.

18. Susan Prillaman (1992), Whole language and its effect on the school library media center. *North Carolina Libraries, 50,* 163.

CHAPTER 5

Results of a Library Survey on Audio Book Materials and Producers

In the summer of 1992, a questionnaire on audio book materials was sent to librarians in 125 small to medium-sized public libraries across the country. The criterion for selection was that a library have a professional position labeled A-V or Media in the 1991 *American Library Directory*. The questionnaire was designed to obtain objective information on six topics concerning audio books that would be of interest to librarians: quality of the reading, sound fidelity and technical quality, durability under use, suitability of the original packaging, price in relation to those of other producers, and replacement policy.

Forty-three usable returns yielded the results reported in this chapter, but not all respondents rated each question or each producer/distributor, which accounts for the varying number of responses shown in the tables below. Respondents rated eight well-known producer/distributors, which we identified on the questionnaire, on a four-point scale: 4 = excellent, 3 = good, 2 = fair, and 1 = poor.

The eight companies rated were Blackstone Audio, Books in Motion, Books on Tape, Brilliance, Cover to Cover, G. K. Hall–Chivers, Recorded Books, and Sterling Audio–Chivers. We encouraged librarians to add additional producer/distributors and to treat all items as open-ended so that they would add comments or opinions. As such subjective or qualitative information can also be valuable to readers, all comments about producers/distributors and all general comments have been included verbatim. Even though they are not quantifiable, these comments show the level of seriousness librarians have in their search for quality products and patron satisfaction.

We have compiled the ratings on the six questions in the form of six

Table 1
Question 1: Rate the Oral Stylistic Quality of the Readings

Producers-Distributors	Rating	Number of Responses	Comments
Recorded Books	3.66	42	Patrons report that RB and GK Hall have the highest caliber readers.
GK Hall-Chivers	3.38	36	See above. GK Hall has richest, warmest, most intimate, most 3-dimensional narration/sound qualities, but several seniors have told me that English accents can be hard to understand.
Books on Tape	3.27	39	B on T is the least favorite in terms of its readers. B on T has least engaging narrators/sound quality - somewhat flat, one-dimensional and even tinny.
Sterling-Chivers	3.2	23	
Books in Motion	3.18	22	
Blackstone Audio	2.89	19	
Cover to Cover	2.8	10	
Brilliance	2.79	29	

Nightingale-Conant	3.67	3	
Audio Book Contractors	3.67	3	
Harper Audio	3.67	3	
Simon & Schuster	3.5	4	
Listen for Pleasure (Durkin-Hayes)	2.63	4	

tables (Tables 1–6) for the producer/distributors listed on the questionnaire. They are arranged by rating, from highest to lowest. Five more companies (Nightingale-Conant, Audio Book Contractors, Harper Audio, Simon & Schuster, and Listen for Pleasure) appear in the tables because each was added to the questionnaire by at least three librarians. A brief discussion of results follows each table. Some general com-

Table 2
Question 2: Rate the Sound Fidelity and Technical Quality

Producer-Distributor	Rating	Number of Responses
Recorded Books	3.71	40
GK Hall-Chivers	3.26	34
Books on Tape	3.22	37
Books in Motion	3.07	22
Sterling-Chivers	3.04	23
Blackstone Audio	2.89	19
Cover to Cover	2.8	10
Brilliance	2.71	28
Harper Audio	3.33	3
Simon & Schuster	3.0	4
Nightingale-Conant	3.0	3
Audio Book Contractors	3.0	3
Listen for Pleasure	2.63	4

ments about producer/distributors included by respondents appear below.

At the end of the questionnaire, librarians were asked to rank different literary genres (Modern Fiction, Mystery, Classics, etc.) according to popularity among their listening patrons. Table 7 presents the rankings and may be useful to school or public libraries that are starting or enhancing an audio book collection.

The questionnaire read as follows:

Check a box for each item under the producers/distributors you are familiar with. On the reverse side are more p/d's and some blank columns which you can label for other companies.

1. Rate the oral stylistic quality of the readings.
2. Rate the sound fidelity and technical quality.
3. Rate the durability under repeated use.
4. Rate the suitability and durability of the original packaging.
5. Did you find the price in relation to other producers to be. . . ?

Table 3

Question 3: Rate the Durability under Repeated Use

Producer-Distributor	Rating	Number of Responses	Comments
Recorded Books	3.34	43	
Books on Tape	3.11	40	
Books in Motion	2.86	22	
GK Hall-Chivers	2.85	36	Worse than poor!
Sterling-Chivers	2.81	21	Too new a product line [to rate]
Cover to Cover	2.7	10	
Blackstone Audio	2.62	21	
Brilliance	2.45	31	
Nightingale-Conant	3.67	3	
Harper Audio	3.33	3	
Audio Book Contractors	2.5	3	
Listen for Pleasure	2.38	4	
Simon & Schuster	2.38	4	

Discussion
Simon & Schuster clearly has a problem with durability as it has dropped to the lowest rating of all producers.

6. If you have dealt with replacement of lost or damaged cassettes, did you find their policy and performance . . . ?
7. Rank the genres in popularity with number 1 the most popular. (Feel free to add categories and numbers.): adventure, classics, modern fiction, mystery, non-fiction, science fiction, self-help, romance, westerns.

General Comments on Producers/Distributors

Blackstone Audio: "Technical services department will no longer let us order from this company because of extra processing required."

Books in Motion: "Number 1: excellent service and product at affordable prices."

Table 4

Question 4: Rate the Suitability and Durability of Original Packaging

Producers-Distributors	Rating	Number of Responses	Comments
Recorded Books	3.27	41	Could use more pictures and color to enhance. Could use some color.
Books on Tape	3.08	40	Drab packaging. Horrible. New packaging.
Books in Motion	2.95	21	
Sterling-Chivers	2.69	21	Worst! Too new a produce line [to rate]
GK Hall-Chivers	2.57	37	Worst Far worse than poor. Their boxes are too flimsy.
Cover to Cover	2.56	9	
Brilliance	2.4	30	
Blackstone Audio	2.4	20	Drab packaging doesn't attract patrons.
Nightingale-Conant	3.67	3	
Simon & Schuster	2.75	4	
Audio Book Contractors	2.67	3	
Harper Audio	2.67	3	
Listen for Pleasure	2.5	4	

Discussion

The raw data about packaging showed a decided anomaly concerning Books on Tape which is not reflected in the table. Some respondents ranked them first, and others much lower. Possible reasons for high rankings include the fact that on their library editions, unique to the industry, they put the name of the library on each cassette. Their current packaging also seems very sturdy. On the other hand it lacks information about the book, author, and reader which are found on Recorded Books and Chivers cases. Books on Tape packages come only in black without illustrations and, until the advent of the library editions a few years ago, their tapes arrived in shipping cartons, totally without information. Some of these may still be on library shelves.

Table 5
Question 5: How Did You Find the Price in Relation to Other Producers?

Producers-Distributors	Rating	Number of Responses	Comments
Books in Motion	3.04	23	
Sterling-Chivers	2.96	23	
Recorded Books	2.93	42	R B are better price [than Books on Tape]
Blackstone Audio	2.8	20	
GK Hall-Chivers	2.76	38	
Brilliance	2.69	29	Excellent on shorter editions
Cover to Cover	2.4	10	
Books on Tape	2.34	38	Very expensive for 2 parts.
Harper Audio	3.67	3	
Simon & Schuster	3.5	4	
Listen for Pleasure	3.0	4	
Audio Book Contractors	3.0	3	
Nightingale-Conant	3.0	3	

Books on Tape: "Good product but pricey." "Books on Tape would do well to do any kind of cover art and a wee bit more information."

Brilliance: "We purchase because it has the most attractive cases."

Cover to Cover: "C to C does not state their policies fully in their catalog."

G. K. Hall–Chivers: Several patrons reported that G. K. Hall does the best job of breaking a tape at the appropriate place and adds directions like, "This is the end of side one," etc.

Listen for Pleasure: "L for P has a terrible catalog. It lacks vital information like price and number of cassettes in a book."

Recorded Books: "RB has good information though art work not extraordinary." "[RB] is producing juvenile color cases now." "RB has a sales representative who is very attentive and helpful." "I like RB and G K Hall catalogs the best."

Table 6

Question 6: Dealing with Replacement of Lost or Damaged Cassettes

Producers-Distributors	Rating	Number of Responses	Comments
Recorded Books	3.37	41	
Books on Tape	3.35	37	
Books in Motion	3.31	16	
Sterling-Chivers	2.72	18	
Brilliance	2.70	23	Best turnaround time of any audiobook company in receiving replacements.
Blackstone Audio	2.63	16	They don't punch tabs on cassette - easy to accidentally record over.
Cover to Cover	2.63	8	
GK Hall-Chivers	2.45	38	Slow with replacement copies. Has been terrible about sending replacement tapes.
Nightingale-Conant	4.0	2	No replacement policy
Audio Book Contractors	3.0	2	No replacement needed yet.
Listen for Pleasure	2.83	3	
Simon & Schuster	2.0	2	
Harper Audio	1.5	2	

Discussion

The changes in Chivers distribution (see chapter 7) may improve replacement response. Note the comments about tabs for Blackstone. Librarians should train their staffs to check for this.

Table 7
Ranking of Literary Genres by Popularity (1 = Most Popular; 9 = Least Popular)

Rank	Genre
1	Modern Fiction
2	Mystery
3	Adventure
4	Romance
5	Non-Fiction
6	Classics
7	Self-Help
8	Science Fiction
9	Westerns

CHAPTER *6*

Annotated Bibliography of Outstanding Titles

This sample collection is meant as a guide to beginning an audio book collection in a public or school library. It may also be used as a selection tool for libraries adding titles. When possible, my selection of books has been based on listening to the book; in these instances, the information category says *listened.* I have also included information that I previously published in various journals, mostly the *Wilson Library Bulletin.* Other information came from the best journals that review audio books: *AudioFile, KLIATT,* and *Library Journal;* these are labelled *review* and a brief citation is furnished. A few titles were selected on the advice of other interested parties; these are labeled *advised.* Where possible, I used information from more than one review. I have tried to include titles from as many suppliers as possible without compromising quality.

In describing this collection I have deviated from industry practice in several ways. In describing a book's format, I do not use the term *unabridged,* because of its negative and misleading connotations; I use instead the term *complete,* for an audio book with the same text as its print version. I do use the term *abridged,* however, though I also may use the term *selections* if the text has not been changed, but discrete units have been excerpted. Also, I round off the price to the nearest dollar; prices are quoted as of January 1, 1993.

In choosing these books, my criteria were intended to produce the most useful and broadly based sampling. First the books labeled *listened* under the *information* category are much more stringently chosen than the others. In most cases they are works that I place at the top of their respective categories and that have been reviewed favorably as well. They are all fully voiced unless otherwise noted. In identifying works that I have not listened to, I have been driven by these criteria, in approximate order of importance: (1) The rating of the reviewer. Most of these books were praised, with little or no criticism. Any criticisms are noted under the category of *disadvantages*. (2) The reader, as some readers are far superior to the average and in fact can turn a mediocre text into an aural tour-de-force. (3) The book itself, as a few readers can work wonders with a weak text, but most cannot. (4) My experience with other audio books that are in some way related. If I have listened to other outstanding books by the same author, reader, or company, I will lean in their direction. (5) The identity of the reviewer, as some reviewers are more discerning than others. I should caution the user of this collection that, in general, audio reviewers tend to be too easy on the works. They are mostly amateurs who may be somewhat intimidated by the only compensation they receive, the often very expensive gift of the audio book itself. Furthermore, the editors of some publications frown on overly critical submissions and are free to delete criticism (see chapter 3 for details).

These reviews are recent for several reasons. Most librarians prefer current material, if only from habit. Recently released titles are more likely to be readily available than backlist items. More important, the art of audio book interpretation has advanced so far and quickly in the last few years that in most cases the most recent titles are the highest-quality ones.

I have tried to cover all of the popular genres, with emphasis upon the more popular ones, as indicated by our poll (see chapter 5); but I have included more *classic* titles, as they seem particularly appropriate to a library collection. The term *classic* supersedes all others. The meaning of most of the data here is self-evident. Under *number,* the ISBN of the recorded book is given if available. Producers who do not make use of ISBN usually create their own order numbers, which in such cases are included instead. I have tried to keep the number of genres to a minimum. The genres in their order of appearance (not frequency) are science fiction, mystery, fiction, classic, young adult fiction, children's fiction, nonfiction, humor, children's classic, storytelling, poetry, radio, and Western. If a title is distributed exclusively in this country by a firm other than the producer, the distributor is given first (under the producer category) and the producer second, in parentheses.

SAMPLE COLLECTION

Author: **Adams, Douglas**
Title: The Restaurant at the End of the Universe
Producer: Dove Audio

Reader: Douglas Adams

Format: complete

Genre: science fiction

Information: review, LJ, 2/1/92

Length: 4 cassettes, 6 hrs.

Cost: $25

Number: 1-55800-294-4

Comments: "The books were meant to be read aloud (the series has also been a radio production and a TV series in Britain), and Adams goes through this incredibly silly tale in an appropriate deadpan."

Author: **Asimov, Isaac**

Title: Murder at the ABA

Producer: Books on Tape

Reader: Daniel Grace

Format: complete

Genre: mystery

Information: review, AudioFile, 12/1992

Length: 8 cassettes, 9 hrs.

Cost: $64

Number: 1054

Comments: "Every so often there is a perfect blend of material and reader, and this is such a case. Grace's nasal superciliousness paints an even better picture of Just than Asimov does on the page."

Author: **Atwood, Margaret**

Title: The Handmaid's Tale

Producer: Recorded Books

Reader: Betty Harris

Format: complete

Genre: fiction

Information: review, KLIATT, 1/1992

Length: 8 cassettes, 11 hrs.

Cost: $59

Number: 88060

Comments: "Very thought-provoking. The reading is done with strong feeling that adds impact."

Author: **Austen, Jane**
Title: Northanger Abbey
Producer: Books in Motion
Reader: Jean De Barbieris
Format: complete
Genre: classic
Information: listened
Length: 6 cassettes, 8 hrs.
Cost: $30
Number: 227
Comments: "Good inexpensive fully voiced version."

Author: **Avi**
Title: The True Confessions of Charlotte Doyle
Producer: Recorded Books
Reader: Alexandra O'Karma
Format: complete
Genre: young adult fiction
Information: review, AudioFile, 9/1992
Length: 5 cassettes, 6.5 hrs.
Cost: $39
Number: 92129
Comments: "Story should be particularly alluring to adolescent girls although the fast-paced action and the nautical setting will also appeal to male listeners."

Author: **Baldwin, James**
Title: Another Country
Producer: Durkin Hayes
Reader: Howard Rollins
Format: abridged
Genre: fiction
Information: review, KLIATT, 11/1992
Length: 2 cassettes, 2 hrs.
Cost: $20
Number: 0-88646-215-0
Comments: "Each character is completely and consistently and believably individualized, and the dialogue is enriched by Rollins's precisely nuanced, on-target inflections."

Author: **Banks, Lynne Reid**
Title: The Secret of the Indian
Producer: Listening Library
Reader: Lynne Reid Banks
Format: complete
Genre: children's fiction
Information: review, AudioFile, 11/1992
Length: 3 cassettes, 3.4 hrs.
Cost: $23
Number: 0-8072-7326-0
Comments: "The breakneck pace of the action and the cliff-hanger chapter endings make this a seat gripper—the audio equivalent of a page-turner."

Author: **Barley, Nigel**
Title: The Innocent Anthropologist
Producer: Chivers Audio Books
Reader: Nigel Barley
Format: complete
Genre: nonfiction
Information: listened
Length: 6 cassettes, 6.5 hrs.
Cost: $54
Number: CAB 659, 0-8161-3189-9
Comments: "Mr. Barley spent two years with the Dowayo people of Northern Cameroon. He reads very movingly, without straining for effects he cannot achieve. The best thing about the book is his unflagging sense of humor, much of it directed toward himself and his profession."

Author: **Barrie, J. M.**
Title: Peter Pan
Producer: Books in Motion
Reader: Patrick Treadway
Format: complete
Genre: classic
Information: listened
Length: 4 cassettes, 4.4 hrs.
Cost: $26
Number: 1-55686-439-6
Comments: "A chance to explore the origins of childhood as a precious state.

His voices are excellent, especially the male ones, and he even gets a hint of Mary Martin into Peter at times."

Disadvantages: "Perhaps due to the lack of Dolby processing this tape (like other Books in Motion productions) may sound different to listeners used to more high tech recordings."

Author: **Barry, Dave**

Title: Dave Barry Does Japan

Producer: Dove Audio

Reader: Arte Johnson

Format: complete

Genre: humor

Information: review, LJ, 11/1/92

Length: 4 cassettes, 6 hrs.

Cost: $25

Number: 1-55800-697-4

Comments: "A medley of hilarious observations and encounters with Japanese culture."

Author: **Bear, Greg**

Title: Blood Music

Producer: Recorded Books

Reader: George Guidall

Format: complete

Genre: science fiction

Information: review, LJ, 4/1/92

Length: 8 cassettes, 11 hrs.

Cost: $59

Number: 91423

Comments: "Complex blend of biological detail and suspense works well in audio."

Title: **Beowulf**

Producer: Recorded Books

Reader: George Guidall

Format: complete

Genre: classic

Information: review, LJ, 5/1/92

Length: 3 cassettes, 3.5 hrs.

Cost: $22

Number: 90053

Comments: "The listener can easily forget that this is an assigned reading and may actually enjoy the experience."

Author: **various**

Title: Best of Science Fiction and Fantasy

Producer: Dove Audio

Reader: various

Format: complete

Genre: science fiction

Information: review, LJ, 2/15/92

Length: 4 cassettes, 6 hrs.

Cost: $25

Number: 1-55800-388-6

Comments: "Range of styles is vast, both in terms of story and narration."

Author: **various**

Title: Best-Loved Stories Told at the National Storytelling Festival, Vols. I and II

Producer: National Storytelling Press (Division of The National Association for the Preservation and Perpetuation of Storytelling)

Reader: various

Format: live

Genre: storytelling

Information: listened

Length: 1 cassette, 1 hr.

Cost: $10

Number: 1-879991-04-7 and 1-879991-05-5

Comments: "A 'greatest hits' compilation recorded live over a number of years at the Festival. It is full of wonderful well-told stories. The sound quality is outstanding since the tapes have been remastered and the crowd noise relegated to the background. Plus the packaging is suitable for circulation."

Title: **Bible (King James)**

Producer: Bible Alliance, Inc. P.O. Box 621, Bradenton, FL 34206

Reader: unidentified

Format: New Testament complete, Old abridged

Genre: classic

Information: listened

Length: not given

Cost: free

Comments: "The Bible in the good listening, hard to read, King James version. OK reading. Also available in other languages."

Disadvantages: "Musical introductions. Technical quality not the best."

Author: **Bodett, Tom**

Title: Growing Up, Growing Old, and Going Fishing at the End of the Road

Producer: Bantam Audio Publishing

Reader: Tom Bodett

Format: selections

Genre: fiction

Information: listened

Length: 2 cassettes, 3 hrs.

Cost: $16

Number: 0-553-47018-3

Comments: "This private world of Homer, Alaska, is actually a real place, but one which is otherwise similar to those created by more traditional storytellers. The impact of the Alaska oil spill upon the town gives Bodett's usual hangdog presentation more genuine pathos than usual. The spare piano accompaniment by Johnny B. also seems like a storytelling characteristic."

Author: **Borland, Hal**

Title: When the Legends Die

Producer: Recorded Books

Reader: Norman Dietz

Format: complete

Genre: fiction

Information: review, AudioFile, 11/1992

Length: 8 cassettes, 10.75 hrs.

Cost: $59

Number: 91208

Comments: "A wonderful addition to high school units on the Native American experience."

Author: **Bradbury, Ray**

Title: Green Shadows, White Whale

Producer: Random Audio

Reader: Ray Bradbury

Format: abridged

Genre: science fiction

Information: review, AudioFile, 9/1992

Length: 2 cassettes, 3 hrs.

Cost: $16

Number: 0-679-41201-8

Comments: "Semi-autobiographical novel of his visit to Ireland to work with John Huston on the script of 'Moby Dick.' This fast-paced audio is a tour de force."

Author: **Braun, Lillian Jackson**

Title: The Cat Who Ate Danish Modern

Producer: Recorded Books

Reader: George Guidall

Format: complete

Genre: mystery

Information: review, LJ, 5/1/92

Length: 4 cassettes, 5 hrs.

Cost: $32

Number: 90081

Comments: "Full of off-the-wall artists with strange habits and exotic beauties, this slyly delightful tale is quite entertaining."

Author: **Brett, Simon**

Title: Mrs. Pargeter's Package

Producer: Dual Dolphin (Isis/Oasis Audio Books)

Reader: Simon Brett

Format: complete

Genre: mystery

Information: review, AudioFile, 12/1992

Length: 6 cassettes, 6.5 hrs.

Cost: $47

Number: 50075C

Comments: "Brett voices his characters with subtle changes of pitch and tone."

Author: **Brown, Dee**

Title: Hear That Lonesome Whistle Blow

Producer: Recorded Books

Reader: Nelson Runger

Format: complete

Genre: nonfiction

Information: review, LJ, 1/1992

Length: 8 cassettes, 11 hrs.

Cost: $59

Number: 91205

Comments: "Fragmented and anecdotal in book form but superb as an audio book."

Author: **Burke, James Lee**

Title: Black Cherry Blues

Producer: Simon & Schuster Audioworks

Reader: Will Patton

Format: abridged

Genre: fiction

Information: review, KLIATT, 9/1992

Length: 2 cassettes, 3 hrs.

Cost: $16

Number: 0-671-73610-8

Comments: "Southern accents are rarely dramatized well, especially the quirky Cajun-French patois spoken in Robicheaux's stomping ground, but South Carolinian Patton does it superbly, with not one false note. The understated music works well, also; this is a first-rate audio production."

Author: **Burnett, Frances Hodgson**

Title: The Secret Garden

Producer: Audio Editions/Spoken Arts

Reader: Susan Fitzgerald

Format: complete

Genre: children's classic

Information: review, AudioFile, 12/1992

Length: 6 cassettes, 7.8 hrs.

Cost: $30

Number: 0-945353-68-5

Comments: "Masterfully interpreting the score of this lovely work, Fitzgerald celebrates the melodious language of Yorkshire and projects living characters through her musical speech."

Author: **Cannell, Dorothy**

Title: The Thin Woman

Producer: Bantam

Reader: Amanda Donohoe

Format: abridged

Genre: mystery

Information: review, AudioFile 11/1992

Length: 2 cassettes, 3 hrs.

Cost: $16

Number: 0-553-47062-0

Comments: "Overplays the accents to almost caricature, but the quirky story can take it. The pace is rapid and action condensed, possibly by the abridgment, so the presentation entertains for its short duration. Femmes Fatales, a sequel, also read by Donohoe is available from Bantam."

Author: **Card, Orson Scott**

Title: Seventh Son

Producer: The Literate Ear

Reader: Orson Scott Card

Format: complete

Genre: fiction

Information: review, AudioFile, 6/1992

Length: 5 cassettes, 7.5 hrs.

Cost: $24

Number: 1-56544-018-8

Comments: "Card is a very good narrator, expressive and well-paced. One can hear the excitement of an author as he brings his own well-described characters to life."

Author: **Card, Orson Scott, and Michael Greenberg (editors)**

Title: The Best Horror Stories of the Year 1988

Producer: Dercum Press

Reader: various

Format: selections

Genre: fiction

Information: review, AudioFile, 12/1992

Length: 4 cassettes, 6 hrs.

Cost: $25

Number: 1-55656-145-8

Comments: "Card's introduction to the collection, as well as his intercalary remarks, are brief and appropriate, and his extended addendum to his own story defines and enlarges it."

Author: **Cather, Willa**

Title: O Pioneers

Producer: Blackstone Audio

Reader: Katherine Yarmen

Format: complete

Genre: classic

Information: review, KLIATT, 11/1992

Length: 5 cassettes, 7.5 hrs.

Cost: $30

Number: 1081

Comments: "This audio would be appropriate not only for pleasure listening, but also in association with courses on American history and women's studies. Yarmen's reading is one of the best I have heard on audiotape! Her tempo and modulation are especially noteworthy."

Author: **Cauthen, John**

Title: Chasing the Wind

Producer: NorthStar Audio

Reader: Dick Taylor

Format: complete

Genre: fiction

Information: review, AudioFile, 11/1992

Length: 7 cassettes, 10.5 hrs.

Cost: $29

Number: 326

Comments: "Taylor keeps the story entertaining and injects life into a novel with limited appeal."

Author: **Cervantes, Miguel**

Title: Don Quixote

Producer: Books On Tape

Reader: David Case

Format: complete

Genre: classic

Information: review, KLIATT, 9/1992

Length: 27 cassettes, 40.5 hrs.

Cost: $216

Number: 2509A and B

Comments: "Case is a wonderful reader in all respects. He is consistent in his use of a wide range of voices and he reads with feeling."

Author: **Ciardi, John**

Title: What Is a Poem?

Producer: Spoken Arts

Reader: John Ciardi

Format: complete

Genre: nonfiction

Information: review, KLIATT, 11/1992

Length: 1 cassette, .5 hr.

Cost: $11

Number: 0-8045-1115-2

Comments: "Side one describes metrics and rhythm; side two deals with how a poem is language-driven, as opposed to being an expression of a poet's preformed ideas . . . totally understandable and also entertaining as he tells in detail how one of his own poems came into being."

Author: **Cisneros, Sandra**

Title: The House on Mango Street and Woman Hollering Creek

Producer: Random House Audiobooks

Reader: Sandra Cisneros

Format: abridged

Genre: fiction

Information: review, KLIATT, 9/1992

Length: 2 cassettes, 3 hrs.

Cost: $16

Number: 0-679-41210-7

Comments: "One of our Hispanic students . . . felt that because of style, accuracy of content, portrayal of male/female relationships, and need for materials depicting the Hispanic background and lifestyle, Cisneros should be in every high school library in both tape and book formats."

Author: **Clancy, Tom**

Title: Clear and Present Danger

Producer: Brilliance

Reader: J. C. Howe

Format: complete

Genre: fiction

Information: review, KLIATT, 11/1992

Length: 16 cassettes, 24 hrs.

Cost: $163

Number: 0-56100-017-5

Comments: "Howe portrays the various characters well and gives an excellent reading. Despite the listening length I was continually caught up in the story and hated to see it end."

Author: **Clark, Mary Higgins**

Title: All Around the Town

Producer: Simon & Schuster Audioworks

Reader: Kate Nelligan

Format: abridged

Genre: fiction

Information: review, KLIATT, 11/1992

Length: 2 cassettes, 3 hrs.

Cost: $17

Number: 0-671-77845-5

Comments: "The abridgment itself lacked only the understanding of Laurie's boyfriend's place in the story, but this was a minor flaw."

Author: **Cook, Thomas H.**

Title: Flesh and Blood

Producer: Sterling Audio

Reader: Peter Whitman

Format: complete

Genre: mystery

Information: review, LJ, 3/15/92

Length: 8 cassettes, 10.25 hrs.

Cost: $65

Number: 1-56054-964-5

Comments: "Recommended."

Author: **Cornwell, Patricia**

Title: All That Remains

Producer: Brilliance

Reader: Sheila Hart

Format: complete

Genre: mystery

Information: listened

Length: 6 cassettes, 9 hrs.

Cost: $57

Number: 1-56100-102-3

Comments: "Brilliance's electronic innovations work well as phone calls and at times memories are slightly altered, which adds to verisimilitude. This audio publisher has always been unafraid to try new technologies, sometimes with mixed results."

Author: **Cornwell, Patricia**

Title: Body of Evidence

Producer: Brilliance

Reader: Sheila Hart

Format: complete

Genre: mystery

Information: review, KLIATT, 11/1992

Length: 6 cassettes, 9 hrs.

Cost: $57

Number: 1-56100-091-4

Comments: "Hart's accent is youthful, middle-American, and she makes subtle, distinct voice changes for the many characters."

Author: **Cornwell, Patricia**

Title: Postmortem

Producer: Books on Tape

Reader: Donada Peters

Format: complete

Genre: mystery

Information: review, LJ, 3/1/92

Length: 7 cassettes, 10.5 hrs.

Cost: $56

Number: 2879

Comments: "Laden with forensic details, this mystery is not for the squeamish."

Author: **Cresswell, Helen**

Title: Posy Bates, Again!

Producer: Chivers Audio Books

Reader: Judy Bennett

Format: complete

Genre: children's fiction

Information: review, AudioFile, 11/1992

Length: 2 cassettes, 2 hrs.

Cost: $18

Number: 1-7451-4421-7

Comments: "Enunciation and impeccable timing clarify the idiomatic text so that its unusual words become another aspect of the book's pleasure."

Author: **Cringely, Robert X.**

Title: Accidental Empires: How the Boys of Silicon Valley Make Their Millions, Battle Foreign Competition, and Still Can't Get a Date

Producer: HarperAudio

Reader: Robert X. Cringely

Format: abridged

Genre: nonfiction

Information: review, KLIATT, 4/1992

Length: 2 cassettes, 3 hrs.

Cost: $16

Number: 1-55994-490-0

Comments: "Clear, entertaining, appealing."

Author: **Davenport, Marcia**

Title: Mozart

Producer: Blackstone Audio

Reader: Nadia May

Format: complete

Genre: nonfiction

Information: review, LJ, 4/1/92

Length: 8 cassettes, 12 hrs.

Cost: $45

Number: 1231

Comments: "Has been in print since 1931 . . . audio version features a new foreword by the author."

Author: **Davis, Donald**

Title: Listening for the Crack of Dawn

Producer: August House

Reader: Donald Davis

Format: selections

Genre: storytelling

Information: listened

Length: 2 cassettes, 2 hrs.

Cost: $17

Number: 0-87483-147-4

Comments: "Donald Davis has created a mythological world of his own around the imaginary town of Sulphur Springs, N.C., which bears a resemblance to his childhood home of Waynesville. There are obvious parallels between Sulphur Springs and the more famous Lake Wobegon. Perhaps the best of the current crop of mainstream storytellers."

Author: **Davis, Patti**

Title: The Way I See It

Producer: Dove Audio

Reader: Patti Davis

Format: abridged

Genre: nonfiction

Information: review, LJ, 10/1/92

Length: 2 cassettes, 3 hrs.

Cost: $17

Number: 1-55800-694-X

Comments: "A unique glimpse into the life of Ronald and Nancy Reagan's daughter."

Author: **de Quincey, Thomas**

Title: Confessions of an English Opium Eater

Producer: Books on Tape

Reader: Thomas Whitworth

Format: complete

Genre: nonfiction

Information: review, KLIATT, 9/1992

Length: 4 cassettes, 4 hrs.

Cost: $32

Number: 2937

Comments: "The charm and humor of the narrative lie in the illumination of De Quincey's personality, at times insufferably elitist, at other times wonderfully tender and human. Repeated listening to this production made for growing enjoyment and appreciation."

Author: **Densmore, John**

Title: Riders on the Storm

Producer: Seven Wolves

Reader: John Densmore

Format: complete

Genre: nonfiction

Information: review, LJ, 3/15/92

Length: 8 cassettes, 11 hrs.

Cost: $32

Number: 0-9627387-9-4

Comments: "Offers irrefutable proof that the audio version can occasionally eclipse its printed cousin."

Author: **Dickens, Charles**

Title: A Christmas Carol

Producer: Recorded Books

Reader: Frank Muller

Format: complete

Genre: classic

Information: review, KLIATT, 11/1992

Length: 2 cassettes, 3 hrs.

Cost: $18

Number: 80200

Comments: "Muller is an American actor but his appropriate, tame simulation of British accents will suit American listeners . . . a wonderfully spooky reading of a short story."

Author: **Dickens, Charles**

Title: Great Expectations

Producer: Chivers Audio Books (Cover to Cover)

Reader: Martin Jarvis

Format: complete

Genre: classic

Information: listened

Length: 13 cassettes, 17.5 hrs.

Cost: $95

Number: 1-85549-055-2

Comments: "A very speedy British version. I especially liked the way Jarvis created Joe Gargery, to my mind the most important character in the story as he represents the natural man in all his virtues and faults. In general the best dialect work I have ever heard."

Disadvantages: "Can be difficult to understand. Priced much higher than the also very good Books in Motion version."

Author: **Dillard, Annie**

Title: The Living

Producer: HarperAudio

Reader: Lawrence Luckinbill

Format: abridged

Genre: fiction

Information: review, AudioFile, 9/1992

Length: 4 cassettes, 6 hrs.

Cost: $25

Number: 1-55994-608-3

Comments: "Luckinbill's graceful, expressive tones give full value to the intensity of Dillard's drama and the subtle details of her poetic imagery."

Author: **Dostoyevsky, Fyodor**

Title: Crime and Punishment

Producer: Recorded Books

Reader: George Guidall

Format: complete

Genre: classic

Information: review, LJ, 4/15/92, also KLIATT, 9/1992

Length: 18 cassettes, 25.5 hrs.

Cost: $117

Number: 91317

Comments: "If the evil in the novel makes one shudder, the effect is mild compared to that of listening to it being described vividly on tape. An overwhelming dramatic performance. Listeners may find themselves looking around frantically for people to forgive us. Not to be missed. FM is dead, all things are permitted."

Author: **Doyle, Arthur Conan**

Title: Sherlock Holmes Stories, Vol. 1

Producer: Books in Motion

Reader: Tim Behrens

Format: selections

Genre: classic

Information: review, KLIATT, 11/1992

Length: 6 cassettes, 6 hrs.

Cost: $34

Number: 1-55686-301-2

Comments: "His dramatization provides the voice changes called for and his judicious deletion of most of the 'he said's' and 'suddenly's' make the readings flow quite nicely. I wanted to know more of Behrens and was disappointed to find nothing about him on the cover."

Author: **Doyle, Arthur Conan**

Title: Tales of Terror

Producer: Books in Motion

Reader: Tim Behrens

Format: selections

Genre: classic

Information: review, AudioFile, 9/1992

Length: 2 cassettes, 2 hrs.

Cost: $15

Number: 1-55686-421-3

Comments: "The characters emerge and speak almost, it seems, independently from the reader."

Author: **du Maurier, Daphne**

Title: Rebecca

Producer: Recorded Books

Reader: Alexandra O'Karma

Format: complete

Genre: classic

Information: review, KLIATT, 9/1992

Length: 11 cassettes, 15.5 hrs.

Cost: $82

Number: 88340

Comments: "The quality narration was captivating from the first moment and should be equally appealing to first-time listeners."

Author: **Estleman, Loren**

Title: Aces and Eights

Producer: Recorded Books

Reader: Joel Fabiani

Format: complete

Genre: fiction

Information: review, KLIATT, 9/1992

Length: 5 cassettes, 6.75 hrs.

Cost: $39

Number: 91418

Comments: "The narrator has an uncanny ability to imitate numerous voices, moods, and inflections."

Author: **Faludi, Susan**

Title: Backlash

Producer: The Publishing Mills

Reader: Susan Faludi

Format: abridged

Genre: nonfiction

Information: listened

Length: 4 cassettes, 6 hrs.

Cost: $25

Number: 1-879371-24-3

Comments: "The cultural analysis of clothing and fashion as well as the manipulation of the legal system by men to the detriment of women are especially revealing. The audio version will not only take the message to many more people, it may lead listeners to the book."

Disadvantages: "Faludi is an adequate reader, and the listener can sympathize when words like 'obstetrics' give her pause. However, the book begins with entirely too many statistics."

Author: **Ferrars, Elizabeth**

Title: Fear the Light

Producer: Chivers Audio Books

Reader: David Rintoul

Format: complete

Genre: mystery

Information: review, AudioFile, 11/1992

Length: 6 cassettes, 6.15 hrs.

Cost: $49

Number: 0-7451-2400-3

Comments: "David Rintoul is a skillful reader who captures nuances of personality with clever intonation and a fine range of accents."

Author: **Ferris, Timothy**
Title: The Mind's Sky
Producer: Dove Audio
Reader: Timothy Ferris
Format: complete
Genre: nonfiction
Information: review, LJ, 3/15/92
Length: 4 cassettes, 6 hrs.
Cost: $25
Number: 1-55800-484-x
Comments: "A journey through the labyrinths of the human brain via the universe."

Author: **Fisher, Carrie**
Title: Postcards from the Edge
Producer: Dove Audio
Reader: Carrie Fisher
Format: abridged
Genre: fiction
Information: review, KLIATT, 9/1992
Length: 2 cassettes, 2.5 hrs.
Cost: $16
Number: 1-55800-088-7
Comments: "Fisher is witty, wise and poignant both in writing and reading."

Author: **Flagg, Fannie**
Title: Daisy Fay and the Miracle Man
Producer: Random House Audio Publishing
Reader: Fannie Flagg
Format: abridged
Genre: fiction
Information: listened
Length: 2 cassettes, 2 hrs.
Cost: $16
Number: 0-679-41025-2
Comments: "This is a transcript of the adolescent D. Fay's diary and therefore all in her voice. The reading flies from one episode to the next with no time for reflection or sorrow."

Author: **Flaubert, Gustave**
Title: Madame Bovary
Producer: Recorded Books
Reader: Davina Porter
Format: complete
Genre: classic
Information: review, LJ, 4/1/90
Length: 9 cassettes, 13 hrs.
Cost: $68
Number: 89393
Comments: "The single best spoken word performance available."

Author: **Follett, Ken**
Title: The Man from St. Petersburg
Producer: Recorded Books
Reader: Simon Prebble
Format: complete
Genre: fiction
Information: review, KLIATT, 11/1992 and LJ, 10/1/92
Length: 9 cassettes, 12.5 hrs.
Cost: $68
Number: 92117
Comments: "Actually a love story with psychological and political thriller over-
tones." "Prebble unfolds this tale in wonderful tones that represent each
character and add suspense to the drama. Follett spins a relentless tale, full
of twists, turns, and discoveries."

Author: **Foote, Shelby**
Title: Shiloh
Producer: Recorded Books
Reader: various
Format: complete
Genre: fiction
Information: review, AudioFile, 12/1992
Length: 4 cassettes, 5.5 hrs.
Cost: $32
Number: 92341
Comments: "This is not, strictly speaking, an ensemble performance, much less

a dramatization, because the readers never interact. Each character's monologue stands by itself."

Author: **Foreman, Dave**

Title: Confessions of an Eco-Warrior

Producer: Audio Press

Reader: Dave Foreman

Format: abridged

Genre: nonfiction

Information: LJ, 11/1/92

Length: 2 cassettes, 3 hrs.

Cost: $17

Number: 0-939643-42-1

Comments: "Lays to rest the 'crazy radical' stereotype and explains how and why the organization was founded."

Disadvantages: "Begins in an understated voice, but warms to his topic without ever becoming shrill."

Author: **Forester, C. S.**

Title: The African Queen

Producer: Sterling Audio

Reader: Michael Kitchen

Format: complete

Genre: fiction

Information: review, AudioFile, 6/1992

Length: 6 cassettes, 6.25 hrs.

Cost: $50

Number: 1-56054-966-1

Comments: "The pace of the reading flows resignedly like the Lumbasi River and then boils with the fervor of their plan."

Author: **Forster, E. M.**

Title: A Room with a View

Producer: Chivers Audio Books

Reader: Joanna David

Format: complete

Genre: classic

Information: review, KLIATT, 1/1992

Length: 6 cassettes, 7 hrs.

Cost: $50

Number: 0-7451-5943-5

Comments: "Very proper British narration is excellent."

Author: **Francis, Dick**

Title: For Kicks

Producer: Chivers Audio Books

Reader: Tony Britton

Format: complete

Genre: mystery

Information: review, KLIATT, 9/1992

Length: 6 cassettes, 8 hrs.

Cost: $50

Number: 0-7451-5950-8

Comments: "Britton is a master at capturing the variety of English voices across class and region. Even his shifts for female voices are successful. Altogether well done."

Author: **Franken, Al**

Title: You're Good Enough, You're Smart Enough, and Doggone It, People Like You!

Producer: Bantam Audio Publishing

Reader: Al Franken

Format: abridged

Genre: humor

Information: listened

Length: 1 cassette, .75 hr.

Cost: $11

Number: 0-553-47094-9

Comments: "The ultimate self-help audio is also perhaps the first example of self-referential audio humor and as such is a milestone in the development of the medium. In addition, laughter being the best therapy, it works as relaxation."

Author: **Freedman, J. F.**

Title: Against the Wind

Producer: Brilliance

Reader: David Colacci

Format: complete

Genre: fiction

Information: review, LJ, 4/1/92
Length: 10 cassettes, 15 hrs.
Cost: $90
Number: 1-56100-090-6
Comments: "Terrific yet graphic hard-boiled thriller."

Author: **Frost, Robert**
Title: A Swinger of Birches
Producer: Stemmer House
Reader: Clifton Fadiman
Format: complete
Genre: poetry
Information: review, AudioFile, 6/1992
Length: 1 cassette, 1 hr.
Cost: $9
Number: 0-88045-099-1
Comments: "Rich yet melodic voice."

Author: **Fulton, Meatball**
Title: Dreams of the Amazon (Jack Flanders)
Producer: ZBS Audio Adventures
Reader: various
Format: complete
Genre: radio
Information: listened
Length: 2 cassettes, 2 hrs.
Cost: $20 or 1 compact disc, $30
Number: cassette #TJ1/2, compact disc TJ1/2DC, 1-881137-00-7
Comments: "The producers traveled to Brazil to gather exotic aural data and
    combined this with tasteful and effective electronic music and excellent
    actors. The end product is anthropology-fantasy, with Jack Flanders a laid-
    back Indiana Jones with a sense of humor."

Author: **Fulton, Meatball**
Title: Ruby 3, The Underworld
Producer: ZBS Audio Adventures
Reader: various
Format: complete
Genre: radio

Information: listened

Length: 4 cassettes, 5 hrs.

Cost: $30

Number: R3A

Comments: "High-tech sci-fi bordering on cyberpunk."

Disadvantages: "In order to make the plot comprehensible to radio listeners who may have missed previous episodes, there is a lot of repetition which slows the action."

Author: **Gardner, Craig Shaw**

Title: Batman Returns

Producer: Bantam Audio

Reader: Michael Murphy

Format: complete

Genre: fiction (novelization)

Information: review, KLIATT, 11/1992

Length: 2 cassettes, 3 hrs.

Cost: $16

Number: 0-553-47075-2

Comments: "The story is not a classic or high literature but Murphy's reading is great entertainment for all ages."

Author: **George, Elizabeth**

Title: For the Sake of Elena

Producer: Bantam Audio

Reader: Derek Jacobi

Format: abridged

Genre: fiction

Information: review, AudioFile, 12/1992

Length: 2 cassettes, 3 hrs.

Cost: $16

Number: 0-553-47034-5

Comments: "Accent, inflections and aristocratic timbre all work to create the English setting for the listener."

Disadvantages: "Any confusion between characters is due to the author's convention of giving them several names."

Author: **Gilbert, Bil**

Title: God Gave Us This Country

Producer: Recorded Books

Reader: Nelson Runger

Format: complete

Genre: nonfiction

Information: review, KLIATT, 11/1992

Length: 12 cassettes, 16.75 hrs.

Cost: $87

Number: 91114

Comments: "A convincing argument that the first American Civil War was fought between the red and white North Americans for control of the Ohio Valley and Great Lakes region . . . resonant, well-modulated voice holds the listener's attention. Special efforts were put forth to correctly pronounce Indian names."

Author: **Gill, Brendan**

Title: Here at the New Yorker

Producer: Books on Tape

Reader: Wolfram Kandinsky

Format: complete

Genre: nonfiction

Information: review, KLIATT, 11/1992

Length: 10 cassettes, 14 hrs.

Cost: $80

Number: 1123

Comments: "Kandinsky actually sounds like Gill should sound as a privileged Yale graduate, a beloved son of a physician, an accomplished writer at a sophisticated magazine. Gill's chatty narration is frank, poignant, frequently amusing, and above all, revealing of many great American writers."

Author: **Gilman, Charlotte Perkins**

Title: The Yellow Wallpaper

Producer: Spencer Library

Reader: Claudette Sutherland

Format: complete

Genre: classic

Information: listened and review, AudioFile, 8/1992

Length: 1 cassette, 1 hr.

Cost: $12

Number: 1-56268-002-1

Comments: "Fully realized dramatic performance with a strong musical presence."

Author: **Godden, Rumer**
Title: Coromandel Sea Change
Producer: Sterling Audio
Reader: Sam Dastor
Format: complete
Genre: fiction
Information: review, AudioFile, 12/1992
Length: 6 cassettes, 7.5 hrs.
Cost: $50
Number: 1-56054-915-7
Comments: "Brilliant array of native voices, accents and dialects characterizes the masterful reading."

Author: **Goodall, Jane**
Title: Through a Window
Producer: Books on Tape
Reader: Penelope Dellaporta
Format: complete
Genre: nonfiction
Information: review, KLIATT, 1/1992
Length: 8 cassettes, 12 hrs.
Cost: $64
Number: 2811
Comments: "Almost unbearably poignant in oral format; highly recommended."

Title: **The Goon Show**
Producer: BBC Radio, Mind's Eye
Reader: various
Format: complete
Genre: radio
Information: listened
Length: 4 volumes, 2 cassettes each; each volume approximately 2 hrs.
Cost: $15 each or set for $50
Number: 0-88142-884-1, 885-X, 024-5, 025-3; set is 885-4
Comments: "Everyone's favorite character from this 1950s BBC series is Bluebottle, brought to life by Peter Sellers, who enters near the end of each show to provide low humor and bring the action to a climax."

Author: **Gore, Albert, Jr.**

Title: Earth in the Balance: Ecology and the Human Spirit

Producer: Dove Audio

Reader: Albert Gore, Jr.

Format: abridged; CD is unabridged

Genre: nonfiction

Information: review, KLIATT, 11/1992

Length: 2 cassettes, 3 hrs; 3 CDs

Cost: $16; CD $40

Number: 1-55800-661-3, CD is 1-55800-792-X

Comments: "Gore has a pleasant voice and does a commendable job of reading with overall rhythmic variety, emphasis, and enthusiasm."

Author: **Gould, Stephen Jay**

Title: Bully for Brontosaurus: Reflections in Natural History

Producer: Books on Tape

Reader: Larry McKeever

Format: complete

Genre: nonfiction

Information: review, LJ, 3/1/92

Length: 14 cassettes, 21 hrs.

Cost: $112

Number: 2819

Comments: "Recommended for all natural sciences collections."

Author: **Greene, Graham**

Title: Under the Garden

Producer: The Audio Partners

Reader: Derek Jacobi

Format: complete

Genre: fiction

Information: review, KLIATT, 9/1992

Length: 2 cassettes, 2.25 hrs.

Cost: $16

Number: 0-9455353-62-6

Comments: "A unique story, ideal for audio, and this production is of highest quality."

Author: **Grey, Zane**

Title: Lone Star Ranger

Producer: Books in Motion

Reader: Gene Engene

Format: complete

Genre: Western

Information: review LJ, 6/1/92 and AudioFile, 11/1992

Length: 8 cassettes, 11 hrs.

Cost: $42

Number: 1-55686-394-2

Comments: "Improbable as some of the story is, it comes to vivid and compelling life through the marvelous reading by Gene Engene." "Engene has a choppy vocal style given to unexpected pauses, stresses in odd places, and vocalizations that are not entirely full but inject character all the same."

Author: **Haley, Alex**

Title: The Autobiography of Malcolm X

Producer: Simon & Schuster Audioworks

Reader: Joe Morton and Roscoe Lee Browne

Format: abridged

Genre: nonfiction

Information: listened

Length: 4 cassettes, 4.5 hrs.

Cost: $20

Number: 0-671-79366-7

Comments: "Morton, an excellent African-American actor, stands in for Malcolm X in an eloquent and persuasive fashion. Sections of third-person narrative which serve as bridges between the words of Malcolm as immortalized by Alex Haley are skillfully read in an avuncular manner by Roscoe Lee Browne."

Disadvantages: "This adaptation is done in such a way that most patrons would never know it is not the original—nor would most librarians, because of deficient labeling."

Author: **Hardy, Thomas**

Title: Far from the Madding Crowd

Producer: Chivers Audio Books (Cover to Cover)

Reader: Stephen Thorne

Format: complete

Genre: classic

Information: listened

Length: 11 cassettes, 14.25 hrs.

Cost: $85

Number: 1-85549-070-6

Comments: "This reader is a sort of British Frank Muller. Very passionate. Great pace."

Author: **Heat Moon, William Least**

Title: Prairy Erth

Producer: Simon & Schuster Audioworks

Reader: Cotter Smith

Format: abridged

Genre: nonfiction

Information: review, LJ, 2/1/92

Length: 4 cassettes, 6 hrs.

Cost: $25

Number: 0-671-76058-0

Comments: "Here in enthralling detail are the region's people, history, geology, and ecology."

Author: **Heller, Joseph**

Title: Catch 22

Producer: Sterling Audio

Reader: Peter Whitman

Format: complete

Genre: fiction

Information: listened

Length: 14 cassettes, 19.7 hrs.

Cost: $100

Number: 1-56054-960-2

Comments: "If someone cuts off the listener on the expressway and a few lines are missed, a laugh may be lost but not the thread of the work. Finally, the many weird characters give reader Peter Whitman a chance to show his stuff, and it is hot and diverse."

Disadvantages: "The only downside is the sexism, which is an unfortunate combination of the worst of the 1960s and the 1940s."

Author: **Hemingway, Ernest**

Title: Ernest Hemingway Short Stories

Producer: Listening Library

Reader: Alexander Scourby

Format: selections

Genre: fiction

Information: review, AudioFile, 12/1992

Length: 2 cassettes, 2 hrs.

Cost: $16

Number: 0-8072-3400-1

Comments: (consists of) " 'The Short Happy Life of Francis Macomber' and 'The Snows of Kilimanjaro.' . . . Through volume, inflection and emphasis, Scourby makes the plots easy to follow as interior monologue and dialogue alternate. Both his men and women sound honest and convincing."

Author: **Herriot, James**

Title: Every Living Thing

Producer: Audio Renaissance

Reader: Christopher Timothy

Format: abridged

Genre: nonfiction

Information: review, LJ, 11/1/92

Length: 4 cassettes, 6 hrs.

Cost: $23

Number: 1-55927-209-2

Comments: "Outstanding reading by Timothy who played Herriot in the BBC TV series."

Author: **Hillerman, Tony**

Title: Dance Hall of the Dead

Producer: Recorded Books

Reader: George Guidall

Format: complete

Genre: mystery

Information: review, KLIATT, 1/1992

Length: 5 cassettes, 6.25 hrs.

Cost: $37

Number: 91122

Comments: "As we listen we learn of the great differences between the Zuni religion and the Navaho religion because this is integral to the plot."

Author: **Homer**

Title: The Odyssey

Producer: Recorded Books

Reader: Norman Dietz

Format: complete

Genre: classic

Information: listened

Length: 9 cassettes, 12.5 hours.

Cost: $66

Number: 89396

Comments: "Very low key, let's all sit around the hearth and listen to the bard spin the tale kind of reading. Basically unvoiced."

Disadvantages: "Caution: the translation by G. H. Palmer was published in 1891."

Author: **Howatch, Susan**

Title: Glamorous Powers

Producer: Chivers Audio Books

Reader: Dermot Crowley

Format: complete

Genre: fiction

Information: review, LJ, 4/15/92

Length: 16 cassettes, 20.25 hrs.

Cost: $110

Number: 0-7451-6042-5

Comments: "A compelling character study of John Darrow, a psychic Anglican priest whose monastic career is brought to an abrupt end by a vision."

Author: **Hughes, Langston**

Title: Langston Hughes Reads

Producer: HarperAudio/Caedmon

Reader: Langston Hughes

Format: selections

Genre: nonfiction

Information: review, KLIATT, 11/1992

Length: 1 cassette, .9 hr.

Cost: $12

Number: 1-55994-571-0

Comments: "Comments he adds about his own life as a Black American contribute to the listener's understanding of the source of his poetry's power.

Sound quality is excellent. Highly recommended as an introduction to Hughes' poetry."

Author: **Hugo, Victor**
Title: The Hunchback of Notre Dame
Producer: Recorded Books
Reader: George Guidall
Format: complete
Genre: classic
Information: review, KLIATT, 4/1992
Length: 16 cassettes, 22.75 hrs.
Cost: $105
Number: 91224
Comments: "A wide range of voices read with enthusiasm."

Author: **Hurston, Zora Neale**
Title: Mules and Men
Producer: HarperAudio
Reader: Ruby Dee
Format: abridged
Genre: classic
Information: review, KLIATT, 11/1992
Length: 2 cassettes, 3 hrs.
Cost: $17
Number: 1-55994-548-9
Comments: "Filled with humor, wit, and just 'plain common sense,' these meta-
    phorical tales explore the uncertainties of life and the unpredictability of
    human nature."

Author: **Hyde, Anthony**
Title: The Red Fox
Producer: Simon & Schuster Audioworks
Reader: Donald Sutherland
Format: abridged
Genre: mystery
Information: review, AudioFile, 11/1992
Length: 2 cassettes, 3 hrs.
Cost: $16
Number: 0-671-64008-9

Comments: "Sutherland's narrative is a pleasure to hear. . . . The abridgment, written by the author, is smooth and logical though the editing breaks at the ends of sides are not."

Author: **Irving, John**
Title: The Water Method Man
Producer: Recorded Books
Reader: Frank Muller
Format: complete
Genre: fiction
Information: review, KLIATT, 4/1992
Length: 9 cassettes, 13 hrs.
Cost: $68
Number: 91203
Comments: "Madcap zigzag."

Author: **Ivins, Molly**
Title: Molly Ivins Can't Say That, Can She?
Producer: Random House Audio Publishing
Reader: Molly Ivins
Format: abridged
Genre: nonfiction
Information: listened and review, KLIATT, 11/1992
Length: 1 cassette, 1 hr.
Cost: $12
Number: 0-679-41549-1
Comments: "The rare example of an abridged audio of a very good book which is even better on tape. Since the printed book consists of a number of short pieces for newspapers and magazines it is entertaining but finally not satisfying. By choosing the best of the essays and reading them thoughtfully and angrily in turn with a humorous to menacing baritone the production makes the anecdotes, most of which concern the good and bad among lawmakers, especially in Texas, much more effective than on the page." "Highly recommended to those interested in politics, history, civil rights; for beginning and advanced listeners."

Author: **James, P. D.**
Title: An Unsuitable Job for a Woman
Producer: Recorded Books
Reader: Davina Porter
Format: complete

Genre: mystery

Information: review, KLIATT, 11/1992

Length: 6 cassettes, 8.75 hrs.

Cost: $42

Number: 92110

Comments: "She captures the brooding intensity, the intelligence and sense of wonder in the central character."

Author: **Jance, J. A.**

Title: Payment in Kind

Producer: Books in Motion

Reader: Gene Engene

Format: complete

Genre: mystery

Information: review, AudioFile, 6/1992

Length: 8 cassettes, 9.5 hrs.

Cost: $42

Number: 1-55686-410-8

Comments: "Fully voiced narration renders each character distinctively, and the deep voice creates a tone of quiet rumination."

Author: **Joyce, James**

Title: Dubliners

Producer: Recorded Books

Reader: Donal Donnelley

Format: complete

Genre: classic

Information: review, LJ, 2/1/92 and KLIATT, 9/1992

Length: 7 cassettes, 9.25 hrs.

Cost: $52

Number: 91223

Comments: "Since these stories unfold almost entirely through dialogue there could hardly be a better book for audio." "With durable packaging, excellent notes, and the greatly appreciated narrated overview at the beginning, this is an excellent addition to any audio collection."

Author: **Kaminsky, Stuart**

Title: Red Chameleon

Producer: Recorded Books

Reader: Mark Hammer

Format: complete

Genre: mystery

Information: review, AudioFile, 9/1992

Length: 6 cassettes, 8.75 hrs.

Cost: $42

Number: 92107

Comments: "The inexorable pace Hammer chooses is perfect for the police inspector who believes, 'You catch more with patience than with speed.' "

Author: **Keating, H. R. F.**

Title: Go West, Inspector Ghote

Producer: Dual Dolphin (Isis/Oasis Audio Books)

Reader: Garard Green

Format: complete

Genre: mystery

Information: listened

Length: 8 cassettes, 9.5 hrs.

Cost: $62

Number: 1-85089-656-9

Comments: "Defamiliarization gives the book a refreshing point of view. The reader mimics various accents with complete credibility and slows the pace skillfully to heighten the suspense."

Author: **Keillor, Garrison**

Title: Stories

Producer: Penguin-HighBridge Audio

Reader: Garrison Keillor

Format: selections

Genre: storytelling

Information: review, LJ, 9/15/92

Length: 2 cassettes, 3 hrs.

Cost: $17

Number: 0-942110-43-9

Comments: "Wry without being cute, warm but not schmaltzy, and satirical sans viciousness."

Author: **Kerouac, Jack**

Title: The Dharma Bums

Producer: Blackstone Audio

Reader: Tom Parsons

Format: complete

Genre: fiction

Information: review, LJ, 5/1/92

Length: 5 cassettes, 7.5 hrs.

Cost: $30

Number: 1309

Comments: "Expresses the Beat sensibility best and probably has the most lasting significance."

Author: **King, Stephen**

Title: Gerald's Game

Producer: Penguin-Highbridge Audio

Reader: Lindsay Crouse

Format: complete

Genre: fiction

Information: review, AudioFile, 11/1992 and LJ, 10/1/92

Length: 12 cassettes, 13 hrs.

Cost: $35

Number: 0-453-00800-3

Comments: "Time goes by quickly indeed thanks to King's provocative, spooky plotting and actress Lindsay Crouse's enthusiasm, skillful reading, and facility with the voices."

Disadvantage: "This tale, more a psychological study than a horror study, moves excruciatingly slowly and, unfortunately, the audio format does not lend itself to skimming."

Author: **King, Stephen**

Title: Sundog

Producer: Penguin-HighBridge Audio

Reader: Tim Sample

Format: complete

Genre: fiction

Information: review, KLIATT, 1/1992

Length: 4 cassettes, 6 hrs.

Cost: $24

Number: 0-453-00757-0

Comments: "Shiver-up-your-spine-type sound effects."

Disadvantages: "Flimsy cardboard packaging."

Author: **Kite, Bernie**
Title: The Fourth Ace
Producer: Books in Motion
Reader: Gene Engene
Format: complete
Genre: Western
Information: review, AudioFile, 11/1992
Length: 8 cassettes, 9 hrs.
Cost: $42
Number: 1-55686-379-9
Comments: "Engene's vocal characterizations are dramatic and individualistic."

Author: **Koch, Kenneth**
Title: Wishes, Lies and Dreams: Teaching Children to Write Poetry
Producer: Spoken Arts
Reader: Kenneth Koch and students from Public School 61 in New York City
Format: complete
Genre: nonfiction
Information: review, KLIATT, 11/1992
Length: 1 cassette, .75 hr.
Cost: $11
Number: 0-8045-1101-2
Comments: "Children reading poems they have written in the classroom . . . comes with a concise but comprehensive four-page digest of Koch's pedagogical rationale and practical suggestions for implementing it. . . . hearing a real voice rendering the rhythms and dramatic emphases of a poem—especially the reader's own poem—communicates in the most direct way what poetry is, and it makes the listener's own creative juices flow in direct response."
Disadvantages: "The readers' words sometimes are indistinct."

Author: **Koontz, Dean R.**
Title: Hideaway
Producer: The Reader's Chair
Reader: Michael Hanson and Carol Cowan
Format: complete
Genre: mystery
Information: review, AudioFile, 6/1992
Length: 9 cassettes, 14 hrs.

Cost: $40

Number: 0-9624010-1

Comments: "Perfectly suited to Koontz's style."

Author: **Kozol, Jonathan**

Title: Savage Inequalities: Children in American Schools

Producer: Brilliance

Reader: Mark Winston

Format: complete

Genre: nonfiction

Information: review, KLIATT, 1/1992

Length: 6 cassettes, 8 hrs.

Cost: $73

Number: 1-56100-086-8

Comments: "Brilliance offered to 'send a complimentary copy . . . to the state official of the bookseller's choice: governor, state congressman, local superintendent, etc.' "

Author: **L'Amour, Louis**

Title: Bowdrie Follows a Cold Trail

Producer: Bantam Audio

Reader: various

Format: dramatization

Genre: Western

Information: review, KLIATT, 9/1992

Length: 1 cassette, 1 hr.

Cost: $10

Number: 0-553-47053-1

Comments: "A full cast of eight voices, authentic sound effects, and musical interludes make this a great listening experience."

Author: **Le Carre, John**

Title: Smiley's People

Producer: Recorded Books

Reader: Frank Muller

Format: complete

Genre: fiction

Information: review, KLIATT, 9/1992

Length: 10 cassettes, 13.75 hrs.

Cost: $75

Number: 90091

Comments: "Muller's reading makes this a masterful suspense tale for older teens and adults, who will be entranced with his authentic accents and his ability to bring Le Carre's characters to life."

Author: **Lee, Harper**

Title: To Kill a Mockingbird

Producer: Recorded Books

Reader: Sally Darling

Format: complete

Genre: classic

Information: review, KLIATT, 11/1992

Length: 9 cassettes, 13.5 hrs.

Cost: $68

Number: 1-55690-517-3

Comments: "The clear, slow narration evokes the languid southern setting in a pleasing way, and also evokes the racist perceptions and language of the 1935 setting."

Author: **Leonard, Elmore**

Title: Freaky Deaky

Producer: Sterling Audio

Reader: Peter Whitman

Format: complete

Genre: mystery

Information: review, LJ, 3/15/92

Length: 8 cassettes, 9.5 hrs.

Cost: $65

Number: 1-56054-962-9

Comments: "Wonderfully interpreted."

Author: **Leonard, Elmore**

Title: Killshot

Producer: Dove Audio

Reader: Bruce Boxleitner

Format: abridged

Genre: fiction

Information: review, AudioFile, 11/1992

Length: 2 cassettes, 3 hrs.

Cost: $16

Number: 1-55800-156-6

Comments: "Narration is sharp and compelling."

Author: **Levitt, Marc**

Title: Tales of an October Moon

Producer: August House

Reader: Marc Levitt

Format: selections

Genre: storytelling

Information: review, AudioFile, 9/1992

Length: 1 cassette, 1 hr.

Cost: $10

Number: 0-87483-209-8

Comments: "His style is distinctive, his voice clear and well-modulated, his characters fully voiced. Eerie sound effects and music are used extensively and appropriately."

Author: **Lewis, Michael**

Title: The Money Culture

Producer: Books on Tape

Reader: Jonathan Reese

Format: complete

Genre: nonfiction

Information: review, LJ, 11/1/92

Length: 6 cassettes, 9 hrs.

Cost: $48

Number: 3020

Comments: "Jargon-free and can be enjoyed by those with only a passing interest in Wall Street."

Author: **Lindsey, David**

Title: Mercy

Producer: Bantam Audio

Reader: Judith Ivey

Format: abridged

Genre: fiction

Information: review, KLIATT, 9/1992

Length: 2 cassettes, 3 hrs.

Cost: $16

Number: 0-553-47042-6

Comments: "Little seems lost in abridgment."

Author: **Lippman, Walter**

Title: Understanding Islam

Producer: Blackstone Audio

Reader: Nadia May

Format: complete

Genre: nonfiction

Information: listened

Length: 5 cassettes, 7.5 hrs.

Cost: $30

Number: 1109

Comments: "A book more likely to be listened to than read, and as such would be an excellent addition to any audio collection. If the Japanese are the group we understand least, Moslems in general are the group we misunderstand most. This book is an excellent primer on the history, social mores, fringe groups, and laws of the divergent congregations with emphasis upon the Arabs and Arabic-speaking peoples."

Disadvantages: "The technical quality of the tape is about B− with noticeable changes in tone quality and even some static."

Author: **Lively, Penelope**

Title: Passing On

Producer: Dual Dolphin (Isis/Oasis Audio Books)

Reader: Sheila Mitchell

Format: complete

Genre: fiction

Information: review, AudioFile, 12/1992

Length: 7 cassettes, 7 hrs.

Cost: $55

Number: 1-8509-786-7

Comments: "Numerous interior monologues are superbly rendered. Because the story is very intimate, the reader's interpretation makes this work a truly moving listening experience."

Author: **Llewellyn, Richard**

Title: How Green Was My Valley

Producer: Chivers Audio Books
Reader: Philip Madoc
Format: complete
Genre: classic
Information: review, LJ, 9/15/92
Length: 12 cassettes, 16.25 hrs.
Cost: $90
Number: 0-7451-6106-5
Comments: "One of the best books you'll ever listen to."

Author: **London, Jack**
Title: Burning Daylight
Producer: Books in Motion
Reader: Tim Behrens
Format: complete
Genre: classic
Information: review, LJ, 6/1/92
Length: 12 cassettes, 13 hrs.
Cost: $57
Number: 1-55686-357-8
Comments: "Behrens captures all the narrator's rambunctious, vicious, tender qualities."

Author: **London, Jack**
Title: To Build a Fire
Producer: Spencer Library
Reader: George Gonneau
Format: complete
Genre: fiction
Information: review, AudioFile, 11/1992
Length: 1 cassette, 1 hr.
Cost: $12
Number: 1-56268-001-3
Comments: "This audio presentation is fully scored with music which could easily stand alone and is narrated to perfection."

Author: **Maclean, Norman**
Title: A River Runs Through It
Producer: Audio Partners

Reader: Ivan Doig

Format: complete

Genre: fiction

Information: review, LJ, 10/1/92

Length: 3 cassettes, 4 hrs.

Cost: $25

Number: 0-939643-41-3

Comments: "Sad and funny, the story is told in a conversational style that readily lends itself to audio."

Author: **Mahy, Margaret**

Title: The Haunting

Producer: Chivers Audio Books

Reader: Richard Mitchley

Format: complete

Genre: children's fiction

Information: review, AudioFile, 9/1992

Length: 3 cassettes, 3.5 hrs.

Cost: $22

Number: 0-7451-8532-0

Comments: "Supple voice and lively pacing combine to create a middle ground—neither wholly real nor entirely imaginary—where Mahy's characters weave their subtly shifting patterns of relationships imperceptibly changed by death and birth."

Author: **Matthiessen, Peter**

Title: Killing Mister Watson

Producer: Recorded Books

Reader: various

Format: complete

Genre: fiction

Information: listened

Length: 12 cassettes, 17 hrs.

Cost: $87

Number: 91320

Comments: "Recorded Books, faced with an excellent novel with a very unusual structure, has created a new format for the audio book. Despite the multiple narrators, this is not a dramatization. Each chapter has a different character and a different reader as narrator, though some characters and all the readers take multiple turns, and sections of nonfiction are interspersed.

The result is unique and quite challenging. The fact that the listener cannot look back as a reader can and figure out the new narrator's relationship to the others and to the story makes hearing this something of a mnemonic exercise, but detracts little from the overall effect. However, the interpretations are mostly unvoiced."

Disadvantages: "It would be somewhat less difficult and even more rewarding if the endpaper maps were included. Recommended for larger collections and adventurous listeners."

Author: **Mayle, Peter**

Title: A Year in Provence

Producer: Audio Renaissance Tapes

Reader: Peter Mayle

Format: abridged

Genre: nonfiction

Information: review, KLIATT, 1/1992

Length: 2 cassettes, 3 hrs.

Cost: $16

Number: 1-55927-170-1

Comments: "Tells it very well indeed with appropriate accents, light humor, occasional understandable exasperation and frustration."

Disadvantages: "Package may survive a few circulations before disintegration."

Author: **McCaig, Donald**

Title: Nop's Trials

Producer: Recorded Books

Reader: Nelson Runger

Format: complete

Genre: fiction

Information: review, LJ, 5/1/92

Length: 7 cassettes, 9.5 hrs.

Cost: $52

Number: 91412

Comments: "In less-skilled hands this might have become overly sentimental or anthropomorphic."

Author: **McCammon, Robert**

Title: Boy's Life

Producer: Simon & Schuster Audioworks

Reader: Richard Thomas

Format: abridged

Genre: fiction

Information: review, KLIATT, 9/1992

Length: 2 cassettes, 3 hrs.

Cost: $16

Number: 0-671-76014-9

Comments: "Considering the possible audience and the reasonableness of the price in this time of budget cuts, this abridgement may make sense."

Author: **McCrumb, Sharyn**

Title: Highland Laddie Gone

Producer: Recorded Books

Reader: Davina Porter

Format: complete

Genre: mystery

Information: review, AudioFile, 12/1992

Length: 5 cassettes, 6.25 hrs.

Cost: $39

Number: 92220

Comments: "Successfully combines light romance, mystery and social satire."

Disadvantages: "British accent . . . is problematic because some of the murder clues relate to misunderstandings due to the similar, but different, English spoken on either side of the Atlantic."

Author: **McCullough, Colleen**

Title: The Thorn Birds

Producer: Recorded Books

Reader: Davina Porter

Format: complete

Genre: fiction

Information: review, KLIATT, 11/1992

Length: 18 cassettes, 26.5 hrs.

Cost: $115

Number: 91308

Comments: "A magnificent job of modulating her voice to portray each of the many characters. Although the accents are different from American speech, her enunciation is clear and the result is easy to understand."

Author: **McCullough, David**

Title: The Johnstown Flood

Producer: Books on Tape
Reader: Grover Gardner
Format: complete
Genre: nonfiction
Information: review, KLIATT, 11/1992
Length: 6 cassettes, 8.5 hrs.
Cost: $48
Number: 2537
Comments: "A gripping human tragedy, expertly read."

Author: **McMurtry, Larry**
Title: Terms of Endearment
Producer: Recorded Books
Reader: Barbara Rosenblat
Format: complete
Genre: fiction
Information: review, LJ, 4/15/91
Length: 10 cassettes, 15 hrs.
Cost: $75
Number: 90067
Comments: "A brilliant example of how good an audio version can be."

Author: **McPherson, James A.**
Title: Abraham Lincoln and the Second American Revolution
Producer: Books on Tape
Reader: Wolfram Kandinsky
Format: complete
Genre: nonfiction
Information: review, AudioFile, 6/1992
Length: 7 cassettes, 7 hrs.
Cost: $56
Number: 2932
Comments: "Even pacing, precise diction and clarity of tone have the feel of a
  good college lecture."

Author: **Melville, Herman**
Title: Moby Dick
Producer: Recorded Books
Reader: Frank Muller

Format: complete

Genre: classic

Information: listened

Length: 15 cassettes, 21 hrs.

Cost: $102

Number: 87370

Comments: "Muller really brings out the adventure and the horror in this version. It gave me nightmares."

Author: **Michaels, Barbara**

Title: Be Buried in the Rain

Producer: Recorded Books

Reader: Barbara Rosenblat

Format: complete

Genre: mystery

Information: review, AudioFile, 11/1992

Length: 7 cassettes, 10.5 hrs.

Cost: $52

Number: 92106

Comments: "Reading is clear, well-paced and easy to listen to. Michaels's books are vastly popular with library patrons, combining her research skills in history and archaeology with romance."

Author: **Michener, James**

Title: Iberia

Producer: Random Audio

Reader: Philip Bosco

Format: abridged

Genre: fiction

Information: review, LJ, 10/1/92

Length: 2 cassettes, 3 hrs.

Cost: $16

Number: 0-394-58792-8

Comments: "Abridged version transforms Michener's Iberia into an exquisite travelogue that dwells on what is uniquely Spanish in the historical and cultural realms."

Author: **Mitchell, Stephen (editor)**

Title: The Enlightened Mind: An Anthology of Sacred Prose

Producer: Audio Literature

Reader: various
Format: selections
Genre: nonfiction
Information: listened
Length: 2 cassettes, 3 hrs.
Cost: $16
Number: 0-944993-48-6
Comments: "An ecumenical collection of short religious selections."

Author: **Moore, Brian**
Title: The Lonely Passion of Judith Hearne
Producer: Sterling Audio
Reader: Frances Tomelty
Format: complete
Genre: fiction
Information: review, AudioFile, 11/1992
Length: 8 cassettes, 8.75 hrs.
Cost: $65
Number: 1-56054-921-1
Comments: "Narration is perfectly timed, perfectly nuanced. In dialogue each character is drawn sharply, totally."

Author: **Morrow, Honore**
Title: On to Oregon!
Producer: Recorded Books
Reader: Norman Dietz
Format: complete
Genre: young adult fiction
Information: review, AudioFile, 9/1992
Length: 4 cassettes, 6 hrs.
Cost: $32
Number: 92122
Comments: "Plain, colloquial delivery is just right for this fictional account of a thirteen-year-old boy who valiantly leads his six brothers and sisters, one a baby, 'on to Oregon.' "

Author: **Mortimer, John**
Title: Rumpole a La Carte
Producer: Durkin Hayes

Reader: Leo McKern

Format: selections

Genre: mystery

Information: review, LJ, 10/15/91

Length: 2 cassettes, 2.5 hrs.

Cost: $16

Number: 0-88646-27-2

Comments: "McKern, Rumpole in the BBC version, gives a delightful narration."

Author: **Muir, John**

Title: The Yosemite

Producer: Audio Literature

Reader: Michael Zebulon

Format: abridged

Genre: nonfiction

Information: review, KLIATT, 4/1992

Length: 1 cassette, 1.5 hrs.

Cost: $11

Number: 0-944993-25-7

Comments: "Likely to lead the listener to obtain a copy for further reading."

Author: **Munro, H. P. (Saki)**

Title: Beasts and Superbeasts

Producer: Books in Motion

Reader: Laurie Klein

Format: selections

Genre: classic

Information: listened

Length: 2 cassettes, 3 hrs.

Cost: $15

Number: 373

Comments: "This is a precise, light, and full-voice recording, and having it done by a woman is a plus."

Disadvantages: "Laurie Klein doesn't attempt English accents, and therefore the nuances of class and condition so important in this author are lost."

Author: **Munro, H. P. (Saki)**

Title: Tales of the Unexpected

Producer: Dove Audio

Reader: Derek Jacobi

Format: selections from various collections

Genre: classic

Information: listened

Length: 2 cassettes, 3 hrs.

Cost: $15

Number: 1-55800-263-4

Comments: "Derek Jacobi, forever identified with the character of Claudius, provides a wonderful reading of this collection of Saki's tales and character sketches. With Waugh and Wodehouse in revival, Munro would seem to be next. The performance seems bland, but is actually very subtle. Sex, age, and especially class nuances are delightfully well done. Mr. Jacobi squeezes the juice from the surprises without smashing them."

Disadvantages: "The problem is in the packaging, though it is physically suitable. The marketers have taken all the space for ads and left none for titles! This is labeled an abridged recording, but surely the tales themselves are not abridged. Most are so slight that they can stand no trimming. To fail to provide bibliographic information is an insult to the writer, performer, patrons, and librarians. Still, this must be highly recommended for public and school libraries."

Author: **Naito, Hatsuho**

Title: Thunder Gods: The Kamikaze Pilots Tell Their Story

Producer: Blackstone Audio

Reader: Christopher Hurt

Format: complete

Genre: nonfiction

Information: review, LJ, 9/1/91

Length: 6 cassettes, 8.25 hrs.

Cost: $30

Number: 1188

Comments: "Compelling first-hand accounts."

Author: **National Public Radio**

Title: Twenty Years with NPR

Producer: Dove Audio

Reader: Susan Stamberg et al.

Format: complete

Genre: radio

Information: review, AudioFile, 6/1992

Length: 2 cassettes, 2 hrs.

Cost: $16

Number: 1-55800-338-X

Comments: "The selections, even if they don't always work, show the possibilities radio offers."

Author: **Nisker, Wes**

Title: Crazy Wisdom

Producer: Audio Literature

Reader: Wes Nisker

Format: complete

Genre: humor

Information: listened

Length: 2 cassettes, 3 hrs.

Cost: $16

Number: 0-944993-58-3

Comments: "Scoop's holy men are the fools, tricksters, clowns, jesters, and other crazies often found at the edge of organized religion or pioneering their own movements. He quotes from some of the better-known examples of this fellowship and tells anecdotes that stretch from prehistory to Abbie Hoffman. There is a lot of emphasis upon Zen, but the quote that struck me was Gandhi's, 'Truth is God, and not the other way round as commonly stated.' "

Author: **O'Brien, Tim**

Title: If I Die in the Combat Zone

Producer: Books on Tape

Reader: John MacDonald

Format: complete

Genre: nonfiction

Information: review, KLIATT, 11/1992

Length: 6 cassettes, 6 hrs.

Cost: $48

Number: 1840

Comments: "Should be in basic collections of large public libraries and considered supplemental material for school libraries."

Author: **Orwell, George**

Title: Down and Out in Paris and London

Producer: Recorded Books

Reader: Patrick Tull

Format: complete

Genre: classic

Information: listened

Length: 5 cassettes, 6.5 hrs.

Cost: $39

Number: 86480

Comments: "The unique feature here is that RB was unable to find an unexpurgated edition of the book and therefore resorted to restoring the profanity."

Author: **Orwell, George**

Title: Homage to Catalonia

Producer: Blackstone Audio

Reader: Frederick Davidson

Format: complete

Genre: classic

Information: review, AudioFile, 12/1992

Length: 6 cassettes, 9 hrs.

Cost: $35

Number: 1262

Comments: "Sounds convincingly as Orwell might have sounded, even to the occasional use of French-accented Spanish pronunciation."

Author: **Pachter, Josh, and Martin Greenberg (editors)**

Title: The Best Mysteries of the Year 1988

Producer: Dercum Audio

Reader: various

Format: selections

Genre: mystery

Information: review, AudioFile, 11/1992

Length: 4 cassettes, 6 hrs.

Cost: $25

Number: 1-55656-129-6

Comments: "The highlight of this highly recommended collection is Harlan Ellison's own dramatic telling of his 1988 Edgar Award-winning story, 'Soft Monkey,' a truly riveting glimpse of daily survival for a New York City 'bag lady.' "

Author: **Paretsky, Sara (editor)**

Title: Beastly Tales

Producer: Dove Audio

Reader: David Birney, Joseph Campanella, Arte Johnson, and Adrienne Barbeau

Format: selections

Genre: fiction

Information: review, KLIATT, 9/1992

Length: 4 cassettes, 6 hrs.

Cost: $25

Number: 1-55800-297-9

Comments: "While the stories are uneven in quality, the narration can't be beat."

Author: **Paretsky, Sara**

Title: Guardian Angel

Producer: Recorded Books

Reader: Barbara Rosenblat

Format: complete

Genre: mystery

Information: listened

Length: 10 cassettes, 14 hrs.

Cost: $75

Number: 92233

Comments: "I've criticized Recorded Books in the past for overly solemn readings of mysteries, but in Sara Paretsky's Guardian Angel they have a mystery that is amusing but can carry a serious reading. The reader, Barbara Rosenblat, who is appearing on Broadway in 'The Secret Garden,' is heir apparent to the mantle of Flo Gibson, perhaps the best known and certainly the most prolific female reader."

Author: **Pepys, Samuel**

Title: The Diary of Samuel Pepys

Producer: Recorded Books

Reader: Alexander Spencer

Format: abridged

Genre: nonfiction

Information: review, KLIATT, 9/1992

Length: 3 cassettes, 4.25 hrs.

Cost: $23

Number: 91326

Comments: "Apologetically short but skillfully edited to 4.25 hours, this recording captures the essence of the precise writings of a man who was witness to the civil war and restoration in England."

Author: **Peters, Ellis**

Title: Death and the Joyful Woman

Producer: Recorded Books

Reader: Simon Prebble

Format: complete

Genre: mystery

Information: review, AudioFile, 11/1992

Length: 5 cassettes, 7.5 hrs.

Cost: $39

Number: 92227

Comments: "Pacing during narrative passages is consistently suited to the actions or emotions described. This reader clearly understands and appreciates the material and lovingly enhances the crisp, clear prose."

Author: **Pilcher, Rosamunde**

Title: Stories from Flowers in the Rain

Producer: Bantam Audio

Reader: Lynn Redgrave

Format: selections

Genre: fiction

Information: review, KLIATT, 11/1992

Length: 2 cassettes, 3 hrs.

Cost: $16

Number: 0-553-47076-0

Comments: "Redgrave manages to go beyond reading to being there. Her sensitivity to the characters is masterfully demonstrated through her use of rhythmic variety, modulation of voice, and energetic interpretation."

Author: **Pinkwater, Daniel**

Title: Fishwhistle

Producer: Dove Audio

Reader: Daniel Pinkwater

Format: complete

Genre: storytelling

Information: listened

Length: 2 cassettes, 3 hrs.

Cost: $15

Number: 0-553-45246-0

Comments: "Perhaps the most entertaining of National Public Radio's (NPR's) 'commentators.' Beware, however. Dove has released several essentially identical versions of these stories under various titles including 'The Best of' and 'Of Dogs and Men.' "

Author: **Plain, Belva**

Title: Crescent City

Producer: Chivers Audio Books

Reader: Bonnie Hurren

Format: complete

Genre: fiction

Information: review

Length: 12 cassettes, 16 hrs.

Cost: $90

Number: 0-7451-6201-0

Comments: "Sweeping story of love and war focuses on the life of a Jewish immigrant and her struggle for happiness."

Author: **Plain, Belva**

Title: Treasures

Producer: Bantam Audio

Reader: Joanna Gleason

Format: abridged

Genre: fiction

Information: review, KLIATT, 9/1992

Length: 2 cassettes, 3 hrs.

Cost: $16

Number: 0-553-47036-1

Comments: "Best for leisure listening for mature teens and adults."

Author: **Poe, Edgar Allan**

Title: The Fall of the House of Usher

Producer: The Spencer Library

Reader: Lloyd Battista

Format: complete

Genre: fiction

Information: review, AudioFile, 9/1992

Length: 1 cassette, 1 hr.

Cost: $12

Number: 1-56268-000-5

Comments: "Brad Hill has composed an original score which evokes Poe's wonderful, moody prose. Battista has just the right voice and inflection to create the atmosphere of escalating terror. Wonderful sound effects (galloping horses, creaking doors, etc.) reflect brilliant editing."

Author: **Radner, Gilda**

Title: It's Always Something

Producer: Simon & Schuster Audioworks

Reader: Gilda Radner

Format: abridged

Genre: nonfiction

Information: advised

Length: 2 cassettes, 3 hrs.

Cost: $15

Number: 0-671-68361-6

Author: **Rendell, Ruth**

Title: Lake of Darkness

Producer: Chivers Audio Books

Reader: David Suchet

Format: complete

Genre: mystery

Information: review, KLIATT, 1/1992

Length: 6 cassettes, 7.5 hrs.

Cost: $50

Number: 0-7451-6238-X

Comments: "British actor Suchet's fast-paced reading is superb and makes the Lake of Darkness consistently, if darkly, entertaining."

Author: **Rhodes, Elisha Hunt**

Title: All for the Union: The Civil War Diary and Letters of Elisha Hunt Rhodes

Producer: Recorded Books

Reader: Norman Dietz

Format: complete

Genre: nonfiction

Information: review, LJ, 5/1/92

Length: 8 cassettes, 11.5 hrs.

Cost: $59

Number: 91406

Comments: "This is the diary brought to national prominence by the Ken Burns 'Civil War' series."

Author: **Rhys, Jean**

Title: Voyage in the Dark

Producer: Sterling Audio, Thorndike Press

Reader: Natasha Richardson

Format: complete

Genre: fiction

Information: review, KLIATT, 11/1992

Length: 4 cassettes, 4.75 hrs.

Cost: $36

Number: 1-56054-920-3

Comments: "In and out of upper and middle class and cockney British English, French, and American accents and language with ease and convincing authority and in and out of the many characters with consistent skill."

Author: **Richter, Conrad**

Title: The Light in the Forest

Producer: Bantam Audio

Reader: Robert Sean Leonard

Format: complete

Genre: young adult fiction

Information: review, KLIATT, 11/1992

Length: 2 cassettes, 3 hrs.

Cost: $16

Number: 0-553-47047-7

Comments: "A note indicates that this recording is 'based' on the novel, but it is virtually word for word faithful to it. This novel is one overlooked or forgotten by many, but it could be valuable as a springboard to discussions on the futility of thinking that race relations can be considered in the absolute."

Author: **Ross, Gayle**

Title: How Rabbit Tricked Otter and Other Cherokee Animal Stories

Producer: HarperAudio/Caedmon

Reader: Gayle Ross

Format: complete

Genre: storytelling

Information: review, KLIATT, 9/1992

Length: 1 cassette, 1 hr.

Cost: $11

Number: 1-55994-542-7

Comments: "A master storyteller; listeners of all ages will hang onto every word and be drawn into the storytelling circle she creates with her quiet, unobtrusive delivery of these Cherokee legends."

Author: **Rudner, Rita**

Title: Naked Beneath My Clothes

Producer: Penguin-HighBridge Audio

Reader: Rita Rudner

Format: abridged

Genre: humor

Information: listened

Length: 1 cassette, 1.5 hrs.

Cost: $11

Number: 0-453-00804-6

Comments: "An excellent selection for commuters, this work is composed of 19 vignettes or chapters excerpted from her book. Each chapter contains two or three mostly autobiographical post-feminist anecdotes loosely connected by theme. Ms. Rudner not only is very funny but also possesses a unique voice with quite a bit of creative range."

Disadvantages: "Tape hiss is quite obtrusive, probably because of a combination of a low-recording level and cheap tape."

Author: **Rushdie, Salman**

Title: Haroun and the Sea of Stories

Producer: HighBridge Company

Reader: Salman Rushdie

Format: abridged

Genre: fiction

Information: listened

Length: 2 cassettes, 3 hrs.

Cost: $16

Number: 0-453-00750-3

Comments: "This audio version of Haroun and the Sea of Stories is definitely not for children. Whether it is the very fast pace or the abridgment, the first half of the story is difficult to follow. Also, the universe that Rushdie has created is so various and overwhelming that the shifts of scene leave one gasping in the dust. Still, Rushdie does pretty good voices, and this minor literary masterpiece belongs in the oral medium."

Disadvantages: "As this is an authorial reading and perhaps an authorial abridgment, a case can be made for this as another work with the same title. But why can't the publisher inform us that all the words in the book are not on the cassette?"

Author: **Sasson, Jean**

Title: Princess

Producer: Audio Renaissance Tapes

Reader: Valerie Bertinelli

Format: abridged

Genre: nonfiction

Information: listened

Length: 2 cassettes, 3 hrs.

Cost: $17

Number: 1-55927-210-4

Comments: "Even abridged, this is an incredibly full account of the plight of even the most privileged members of the female caste. Not just to honor her courage or because this is a real-life thriller, but because this audio book is a startlingly important document, it should be in every collection."

Author: **Sayers, Dorothy**

Title: Gaudy Night

Producer: Durkin Hayes

Reader: Edward Petherbridge

Format: abridged

Genre: mystery

Information: review, KLIATT, 11/1992

Length: 2 cassettes, 3 hrs.

Cost: $16

Number: 0-88646-284-3

Comments: "Award-winning British actor Petherbridge, familiar to stage audiences from Nicholas Nickleby and to fans of PBS's 'Mystery' as Wimsey in the BBC adaptation of Sayers' novels, differentiates all characters with accents, tone, or mood to suit, and captures the essence of the characters and the times."

Disadvantages: "His haughty British intonation for Peter's voice, typical of the period, may annoy some listeners not used to British upper-class lingo."

Author: **Sayers, Dorothy**
Title: Unnatural Death
Producer: Chivers Audio Books
Reader: Ian Carmichael
Format: complete
Genre: mystery
Information: review, LJ, 4/15/91
Length: 6 cassettes, 8 hrs.
Cost: $50
Number: 0-7451-6262-2
Comments: "Carmichael has performed the role of Lord Peter on TV."

Author: **Scott, Paul**
Title: The Jewel in the Crown
Producer: Books on Tape
Reader: Richard Brown
Format: complete
Genre: fiction
Information: review, LJ, 3/15/92
Length: 16 cassettes, 24 hrs.
Cost: $128
Number: 2871A and B
Comments: "Narration is excellent."

Author: **Serling, Rod**
Title: The Twilight Zone: Walking Distance
Producer: HarperAudio
Reader: Cliff Robertson
Format: dramatization
Genre: fiction
Information: review, AudioFile, 12/1992
Length: 1 cassette, 1.25 hrs.
Cost: $11
Number: 1-55994-660-1
Comments: "Robertson's dynamic reading brings every dimension of this visually charged story vividly to life."

Author: **Shakespeare, William**
Title: As You Like It
Producer: HarperAudio/Caedmon
Reader: Vanessa Redgrave and Rex Harrison plus complete cast
Format: complete
Genre: classic
Information: review, LJ, 6/1/91
Length: 2 cassettes, 2.3 hrs.
Cost: $16
Number: 1-55994-085-9
Comments: "Stellar rendition."

Author: **Shakespeare, William**
Title: Much Ado about Nothing
Producer: HarperAudio/Caedmon
Reader: Vanessa Redgrave and Rex Harrison plus complete cast
Format: complete
Genre: classic
Information: review, LJ, 6/1/91
Length: 2 cassettes, 1.8 hrs.
Cost: $16
Number: 1-55994-098-0
Comments: "Traditional theatrical flavor."

Author: **Shalev, Meir**
Title: The Blue Mountain
Producer: Recorded Books
Reader: George Guidall
Format: complete
Genre: fiction
Information: review, LJ, 10/1/92
Length: 11 cassettes, 16.25 hrs.
Cost: $82
Number: 92116
Comments: "Interpretation is a masterpiece—at times immediate, at other times almost hypnotic, and always true to the European accents and speech patterns of the characters."

Author: **Sheldon, Sidney**

Title: The Stars Shine Down

Producer: Dove Audio

Reader: Roddy McDowell

Format: complete

Genre: fiction

Information: review, AudioFile, 12/1992

Length: 12 cassettes, 9 hrs.

Cost: $50

Number: 1-55800-650-8

Comments: "McDowell captures the dialects of all the Glass Bay tenants, the stammer of Lara's partner, Howard Keller, and the raspy voice of Paul Martin so accurately that a mental image of the characters emerges."

Author: **Shute, Nevil**

Title: Ruined City

Producer: Chivers Audio Books

Reader: Robin Bailey

Format: complete

Genre: fiction

Information: review, LJ, 5/1/92

Length: 6 cassettes, 7.25 hrs.

Cost: $50

Number: 0-7451-6279-7

Comments: "Well-crafted fully voiced reading helps keep the focus sharp throughout."

Author: **Sillitoe, Alan**

Title: The Loneliness of the Long Distance Runner and Saturday Afternoon

Producer: Durkin Hayes

Reader: Tom Courtenay

Format: complete

Genre: young adult fiction

Information: review, KLIATT, 11/1992

Length: 2 cassettes, 2 hrs.

Cost: $20

Number: 0-88646-060-3

Comments: "Courtenay, who starred in the film version of the story, does an absolutely convincing job of inhabiting and projecting the character of Smith, whose witty, cheeky rebelliousness is utterly winning."

Author: **Simms, Laura**

Title: Women and Wild Animals: Howl the Morning Welcome

Producer: Audio Press

Reader: Laura Simms

Format: complete

Genre: storytelling

Information: listened

Length: 1 cassette, 1.75 hrs.

Cost: $17

Number: 0-939643-37-5

Comments: "An outstanding example of storytelling by a performer who collects and reads tales that she then makes into her own. Music by Steve Gorn. Listeners to full voice audio books will be comfortable with this work as Simms creates a voice for each character. Indeed, this New York-based academic storyteller is one of the most expressive and versatile stylists I've heard. These stories reflect the historical feminist or Goddess myth perspective and draw from cultures such as the Kikuyu, Inuit, and Roumanian and include personal interludes. The music is performed on a number of traditional instruments and is wonderfully supportive. But it is Ms. Simms's ability to speak intimately to the listener which makes these recordings special."

Author: **Solzhenitsyn, Aleksandr**

Title: One Day in the Life of Ivan Denisovich

Producer: Blackstone Audio

Reader: Richard Brown

Format: complete

Genre: fiction

Information: review, LJ, 9/15/92

Length: 4 cassettes, 6 hrs.

Cost: $26

Number: 1289

Comments: "Razor-sharp narration."

Author: **Spark, Muriel**

Title: The Prime of Miss Jean Brodie

Producer: Audio Partners, Inc.

Reader: Geraldine McEwan

Format: complete

Genre: fiction

Information: review, KLIATT, 1/1992

Length: 3 cassettes, 4 hrs.

Cost: $20

Number: 0-945353-31-6

Comments: "More like Miss Brodie in retirement than in her prime; this can be forgiven; her hint of a Scots burr perfectly evokes Edinburgh in the '30s and she reads with irony and wit."

Author: **Steinem, Gloria**

Title: Revolution from Within

Producer: Dove Audio

Reader: Gloria Steinem

Format: abridged

Genre: nonfiction

Information: review, AudioFile, 9/1992

Length: 2 cassettes, 3 hrs.

Cost: $16

Number: 1-55800-605-2

Comments: "Straightforward and friendly, but not intimate, presentation."

Disadvantages: "The listener wished the book were unabridged. Steinem left me wanting to learn more."

Author: **Stevens, Stuart**

Title: Night Train to Turkistan

Producer: Books on Tape

Reader: Bill Whitaker

Format: complete

Genre: nonfiction

Information: review, KLIATT, 11/1992

Length: 5 cassettes, 7.5 hrs.

Cost: $40

Number: 2638

Comments: "Quality of narration is excellent and conveys a young energetic tempo. The end of each chapter enticingly leads the reader on."

Author: **Stokesbury, James L.**

Title: A Short History of World War II

Producer: Recorded Books

Reader: Nelson Runger

Format: complete

Genre: nonfiction

Information: review, KLIATT, 4/1992

Length: 12 cassettes, 18 hrs.

Cost: $90

Number: 91204

Comments: "Few students would read this, but this audio book should make the book more accessible."

Author: **Stratton-Porter, Gene**

Title: Laddie

Producer: Books in Motion

Reader: Laurie Klein

Format: complete

Genre: classic

Information: review, AudioFile, 12/1992

Length: 12 cassettes, 14.5 hrs.

Cost: $58

Number: 1-55686-346-2

Comments: "Wonderfully depicts family life on a turn-of-the-century Indiana farm. Interspersed with this simple story is a mystery concerning their new British neighbors."

Author: **Tan, Amy**

Title: The Kitchen God's Wife

Producer: Dove Audio

Reader: Amy Tan

Format: complete

Genre: fiction

Information: listened

Length: 12 cassettes, 18 hrs.

Cost: $40

Number: 1-55800-434-3

Comments: "Excellent authorial reading of a fine book concerning China during World War II."

Disadvantages: "Terrible packaging."

Author: **Thoene, Bodie**

Title: A Daughter of Zion

Producer: North Star Audio Books

Reader: Lois Betterton

Format: complete

Genre: fiction

Information: listened

Length: 9 cassettes, 13.5 hrs.

Cost: $50 (library $40)

Number: 378

Comments: "The climactic scenes of this religion-oriented book (in the ancient cisterns and sewers of the Old City of Jerusalem) match most mainstream thrillers in suspense and realistic detail."

Author: **Thomas, Lewis**

Title: The Fragile Species

Producer: Recorded Books

Reader: George Guidall

Format: complete

Genre: nonfiction

Information: review, AudioFile, 12/1992

Length: 6 cassettes, 8 hrs.

Cost: $42

Number: 9222

Comments: "Guidall's ability to present each opinion as his own, combined with his well-seasoned, mature timbre, make him an extremely plausible and appropriate stand-in for Dr. Thomas."

Author: **Trillin, Calvin (host)**

Title: An Evening with Garrison Keillor, Maya Angelou, Laurie Colwin, Tom Wolf

Producer: Dove Audio

Reader: various authorial readings

Format: complete

Genre: fiction

Information: review, KLIATT, 9/1992

Length: 1 cassette, 1 hr.

Cost: $11

Number: 1-55800-401-7

Comments: "The sound quality is good for a live performance, and the audience is very responsive."

Author: **Tuchman, Barbara**

Title: The March of Folly: From Troy to Vietnam

Producer: Books on Tape

Reader: Grover Gardner

Format: complete

Genre: nonfiction

Information: review, KLIATT, 11/1992

Length: 12 cassettes, 18 hrs.

Cost: $96

Number: 2610

Comments: "Schools may want to use this audio to introduce Tuchman's work, while public libraries should add it to any audio collection."

Author: **Twain, Mark**

Title: The Adventures of Huckleberry Finn

Producer: Books in Motion

Reader: Tim Behrens

Genre: classic

Format: complete

Information: listened

Length: 8 cassettes, 11.2 hrs.

Cost: $42

Number: 1-55686-348-9

Comments: "Books in Motion continues to produce the highest quality American audio books. Only an American actor could read *Huckleberry Finn* with the accurate accents and sensitivity to nuance that Tim Behrens brings to the work. The subtle variations in intonation make it clear he has studied the regional dialects of the middle South, and the Paul Robeson-style bass-baritone used for Jim gives the role a dignity perhaps even beyond Twain's intentions or imagination. First-rate technical quality, along with the highest aesthetic standards and a light comic touch, makes this title a necessary purchase for all libraries with audio book collections, even if they already have one of the run-of-the-mill versions."

Author: **Twain, Mark**

Title: The Adventures of Tom Sawyer

Producer: Books in Motion

Reader: Tim Behrens

Genre: classic

Format: complete

Information: advised
Length: 6 cassettes, 7 hrs.
Cost: $34
Number: 1-55686-110-9

Author: **Twain, Mark**
Title: Carnival of Crime
Producer: The Spencer Library
Reader: Larry Kenney
Format: complete
Genre: classic
Information: review, AudioFile, 9/1992
Length: 1 cassette, 1 hr.
Cost: $12
Number: 1-56268-004-8
Comments: "Laurie Altman's original score of popular riverboat themes and music of Twain's era is performed continuously throughout and in synchronization with Larry Kenney's reading."

Author: **Tyler, Ann**
Title: The Accidental Tourist
Producer: Recorded Books
Reader: George Guidall
Format: complete
Genre: fiction
Information: review, LJ, 4/15/92
Length: 9 cassettes, 13.25 hrs.
Cost: $68
Number: 91404
Comments: "There is much more to this than mere entertainment."

Author: **Underwood, Michael**
Title: Death by Misadventure
Producer: Chivers Audio Books
Reader: Stephen Thorne
Format: complete
Genre: mystery
Information: review, AudioFile, 12/1992
Length: 6 cassettes, 6.2 hrs.

Cost: $50

Number: 0-7451-2402-X

Comments: "Thorne's portrayal of Detective Superintendent Manton makes him come alive."

Author: **Virgil**
Title: The Aeneid
Producer: Blackstone Audio
Reader: Frederick Davidson
Format: complete
Genre: classic
Information: review, KLIATT, 11/1992
Length: 10 cassettes, 15 hrs.
Cost: $54
Number: 1277
Comments: "A modern 'English prose' translation of an ancient Latin poem. Being as accessible a version as one is likely to find, this may be the only way some people will be able to get into such a difficult book."

Author: **Voigt, Cynthia**
Title: Homecoming
Producer: Recorded Books
Reader: Barbara Caruso
Format: complete
Genre: young adult fiction
Information: review, AudioFile, 11/1992
Length: 10 cassettes, 14.25 hrs.
Cost: $75
Number: 92123
Comments: "Narrative style is low-key, like the author's, but it grows on you. Her voice soon becomes an extension of the book, rather than an intermediary."

Author: **Voltaire**
Title: Candide
Producer: Books on Tape
Reader: Tim Whitman
Format: complete
Genre: classic
Information: review, LJ, 5/1/92

Length: 4 cassettes, 4 hrs.

Cost: $32

Number: 2931

Comments: "Dry elocution and marvelous variety of intonations had this reviewer laughing with dismay."

Author: **Vonnegut, Kurt**

Title: Hocus Pocus

Producer: Recorded Books

Reader: Norman Dietz

Format: complete

Genre: fiction

Information: listened

Length: 7 cassettes, 9.75 hrs.

Cost: $52

Number: 91210

Comments: "One more chapter in Vonnegut's one-man war with the establishment, this work was written in a forwards referential style that is very good to listen to. In fact, this book may be better suited to audio than to print. It is a tale of madness, extramarital sex, McCarthyism, and a bloody jailbreak set in the United States of Dystopia, circa 2001. Lots of other interesting food for the mind is included down to a sub-subplot concerning the omnipresent Elders of Tralfamadore."

Disadvantages: "Mr. Dietz does relatively little with different voices, but since the book is about 95 percent first-person narration, this is hardly a limitation. However he does sometimes cross the line from irony to sarcasm, most notably when he renders the narrator's 'cough, cough' by reading it rather than by coughing."

Author: **Walton, Izaak**

Title: The Compleat Angler

Producer: Recorded Books

Reader: Nelson Runger

Format: complete

Genre: classic

Information: review, KLIATT, 1/1992

Length: 6 cassettes, 9 hrs.

Cost: $42

Number: 86920

Comments: "Nelson Runger reads with vigor and with the lighthearted spirit that Walton certainly intended."

Author: **Wambaugh, Joseph**
Title: The Golden Orange
Producer: Brilliance
Reader: George Ralph
Format: complete
Genre: mystery
Information: review, LJ, 10/1/91
Length: 6 cassettes, 9 hrs.
Cost: $73
Number: 1-56100-070-1
Comments: "Great stuff for adult collections."

Author: **Waugh, Evelyn**
Title: Brideshead Revisited
Producer: Chivers Audio Books
Reader: Jeremy Irons
Format: complete
Genre: classic
Information: review, AudioFile, 9/1992
Length: 8 cassettes, 11.4 hrs.
Cost: $80
Number: 0-7451-6346-7
Comments: "Irons's total familiarity with the story reveals itself in a flawless portrayal of a wide range of familiar, complex characters, who include the manipulative Lady Marchmain, the elusive Julia, and the outrageous Anthony Blanche."

Author: **Waugh, Evelyn**
Title: A Handful of Dust
Producer: Sterling Audio
Reader: Andrew Sachs
Format: complete
Genre: classic
Information: listened
Length: 8 cassettes, 6.7 hrs.
Cost: $65
Number: 1-56054-974-2
Comments: "Andrew Sachs played Manuel in Fawlty Towers. Tragic-comic."

Author: **Waugh, Evelyn**

Title: Scoop

Producer: Cover to Cover

Reader: Simon Cadell

Format: complete

Genre: humor

Information: listened

Length: 6 cassettes, 7 hrs.

Cost: $50

Number: 1-85549-021-8

Comments: "This is for my money Waugh's best book, avoiding the extreme cynicism of the earlier works and the sentimentality of the late ones. The reader, Simon Cadell, is perfect not only in his voices but also in his pacing. Some listeners may be nonplussed by the speed of the first chapter, but after having plunged into the chaotic world of London's smart set, Cadell settles down and milks the satire for all it's worth. He even manages to mute the author's racism by making the Africans less obnoxious than they appear on the page, though it would not be possible or true to the book to eliminate this aspect entirely."

Author: **Webb, Mary**

Title: Precious Bane

Producer: Books on Tape

Reader: Jill Masters

Format: complete

Genre: classic

Information: listened

Length: 8 cassettes, 12 hrs.

Cost: $64

Number: 2348

Comments: "The exceptionally lively dramatis personae features a heroine with a 'hare-shotten' lip, a vivid cast of rustic villains, and a noble but credible protagonist. Add to these an ear-opening early Victorian vocabulary and some Hardyesque ideas about the nexus of Christianity and Paganism and the result is a heady homebrew indeed."

Disadvantages: "If your patrons can figure out 'clemmed' and 'very middling' from context then they can enjoy this."

Author: **Weber, Janice**

Title: Frost the Fiddler

Producer: Brilliance

Reader: Sandra Burr

Format: complete

Genre: fiction

Information: review, AudioFile, 12/1992

Length: 8 cassettes, 12 hrs.

Cost: $73

Number: 1-56100-106-6

Comments: "Provides just the right mix of cool calculation and sultry softness to bring Frost's character to life and lures listeners into the story."

Author: **Whitney, Phyllis**

Title: Woman without a Past

Producer: Brilliance

Reader: Joyce Bean

Format: complete

Genre: mystery

Information: review, LJ, 6/15/92

Length: 6 cassettes, 9 hrs.

Cost: $58

Number: 1-56100-093-0

Comments: "Just as one thinks the story is climaxing, it takes off again following another path."

Author: **Williams, Charles**

Title: All Hallows Eve

Producer: Christians Listening Audio

Reader: Dick Taylor

Format: complete

Genre: fiction

Information: listened

Length: 6 cassettes, 9 hrs.

Cost: $39 (library $26)

Number: 317

Comments: "The plot moves quickly, and certain scenes are very well done and at times riveting. Among the best are the magician's attempts to send his illegitimate daughter as an emissary to the land of the dead, the creation of a homunculus in which the protagonist briefly returns to the living, the discussions of art, and of course the final climactic battle between the forces of good and evil."

Disadvantages: "Detailed descriptions of the world of the newly dead and an excessive amount of psycho-religious analysis. Not surprisingly, given Milton's example, the anti-Christ is the most interesting character and the work pales when he is absent."

Author: **Williams, Ursula Moray**
Title: Tiger Nanny
Producer: Chivers Audio Books
Reader: Penelope Wilton
Format: complete
Genre: children's fiction
Information: review, AudioFile, 9/1992
Length: 2 cassettes, 2.75 hrs.
Cost: $18
Number: 0-7451-4418-7
Comments: "Flawless, multiple-voiced reading by British actress Penelope Wilton is smooth, charming and easy to listen to; the story is captivating, and Chivers' attention to detail will leave patrons devoted fans."

Author: **Wister, Owen**
Title: The Virginian
Producer: Books in Motion
Reader: Gene Engene
Format: complete
Genre: Western
Information: review, LJ, 5/15/91
Length: 12 cassettes, 15.5 hrs.
Cost: $58
Number: 1-55686-353-5
Comments: "One of the genre's most enduring titles."

Author: **Wodehouse, P. G.**
Title: Full Moon
Producer: Chivers Audio Books
Reader: Jeremy Sinden
Format: complete
Genre: humor
Information: listened
Length: 6 cassettes, 7.8 hrs.
Cost: $50

Number: 0-7451-6367-X

Comments: "The book is the best-plotted Wodehouse I know, and the slight weakness of Jeremy Sinden's reading allows the characters' strengths to win the listener over. Wodehouse's basic philosophy is revealed here. He continues to appeal because his humor reveals basic truths: the anarchism of youth, the hope of maintaining a youthful outlook into later life, the eccentricities and sheer dottiness of those who succeed, and the dreariness of those who don't."

Author: **Wodehouse, P. G.**
Title: Jeeves Takes Charge
Producer: Buckingham Classics, Ltd.
Reader: Edward Duke
Format: abridged
Genre: humor
Information: listened
Length: 1 cassette, 1 hr.
Cost: $8
Number: 0-929071-20-4
Comments: "Adapted from Duke's stage show."

Author: **Wodehouse, P. G.**
Title: The Mating Season
Producer: Chivers Audio Books
Reader: Jonathan Cecil
Format: complete
Genre: humor
Information: review, LJ, 6/15/92
Length: 8 cassettes, 7 hrs.
Cost: $65
Number: 0-7451 6374-2
Comments: "Super performance . . . renditions of the crotchety aunts are particularly hilarious."

Author: **Wodehouse, P. G.**
Title: Service with a Smile
Producer: Blackstone Audio
Reader: Frederick Davidson
Format: complete
Genre: humor

Information: listened

Length: 5 cassettes, 7.5 hrs.

Cost: $30

Number: 1220

Comments: "Very exaggerated and funny characterizations."

Author: **Young, Richard A., and Judy Dockery Young**

Title: Ozark Ghost Stories

Producer: August House

Reader: Richard A. Young and Judy Dockery Young

Format: selections

Genre: children's storytelling

Information: review, AudioFile, 9/1992

Length: 1 cassette, 1 hr.

Cost: $10

Number: 0-87483-211-X

Comments: "Both storytellers have clear, sinister tones that serve their stories well."

CHAPTER 7

A Critical Directory of Audio Book Producers and Distributors

The information in this section is about individual producers and distributors of complete audio books. The information in each entry is transcribed exactly from questionnaires completed by these companies. Ellipses indicate omissions due to lack of space. At the end of some entries, editorial comment based on my experiences as librarian and reviewer has been added. Any further interpolations are found within parentheses.

As I have tried to include the primary source for all tapes mentioned in chapter 6, many but not all children's, abridged, storyteller, radio, and other producers are incorporated. To supply this information on every available source would require an additional book. Companies mentioned in the text or in chapter 6 that were not sent or did not return a questionnaire are represented by basic information in paragraph form. These data came mostly from company catalogs, though I made phone calls to confirm if necessary. Packaging information in AudioFile style is given if known.

This kind of information is important, because librarians must be aware of sources of good audio books other than the half-dozen largest firms. If prices and quality are to improve, we must spend as much of our budgets as possible on reasonably priced high-quality products.

American Audio Prose Library
P. O. Box 842
Columbia, MO 65205
800-447-2275, 314-443-0361

Producer and distributor

Number of titles available: approximately 700

Relation to the printed version: 50% complete, 50% abridged

Sound/music: sound effects and music

Library discount: no; for a special package of black writers, 25% discount

Genres: adventure, classics, modern fiction, nonfiction, Westerns

Replacement: $7 per cassette

Distribution: Inland Book Company and Ladyslipper

Company focus: We operate as a nonprofit, and our goal is to keep a comprehensive selection of authors available on audiocassette. We also are committed to the works of minority authors and women.

American Audio is a good source for readings of modern American classics, many read by the authors. Mostly short form and selections.

Audio Book Contractors
P. O. Box 40115
Washington, DC 20016-0115
202-363-3429; FAX 202-363-3429
Producer and distributor

Number of titles available: 354

Relation to the printed version: complete

Sound/music: neither

Library discount: yes

Terms: 10% off 50 albums or more, 20% off 100 or more; a few special listings for libraries and schools

Genres: adventure, classics, nonfiction, romance

Replacement: $6 per cassette plus postage and handling, replaced within 48 hours

Distribution: Professional Media Services, Audio Diversions

Company focus: Unabridged classics. All our narrators are professional actors.

Audio Book Contractors is Flo Gibson's personal audio book production company. She is perhaps the premier woman reader. Gibson learned her craft at the Library of Congress and has also recorded extensively for Books on Tape and Recorded Books. Several good readers have worked for her, presumably learned her technique, and then moved on to other companies. The contractor part of the name comes from Gibson's willingness to record books for other distributors, currently Ride with Me. Bookpak.

Audio Editions: see Audio Partners

Audio Oddities
5062 S. 108th St. #108
Omaha, NE 681371
402-896-8105
Producer and distributor

Number of titles available: 5

Relation to the printed version: 60% complete, 40% abridged

Sound/music: sound effects and music

Library discount: no

Genres: adventure, nonfiction, Westerns

Replacement: At original price

Company focus: Multiple voices dramatize the material.

Audio Partners produces and distributes audio books as Audio Editions Books on Cassette and is in turn distributed by Publishers Group West. Both Partners and Editions are located at P. O. Box 6930, 1133 High St., Auburn, CA 95603. Phone numbers are 800-231-4261, 916-888-7803 and 7801, FAX 916-888-7805. The number 800-788-3123 reaches Publishers Group West only. Newman Audio is a defunct imprint of Audio Editions. Most titles are abridged.

Audio Press/Northword Press, Inc.
P. O. Box 1360 7520 Hwy. 51 S.
Minocqua, WI 54548
715-356-9800, 800-336-5666
Producer and distributor

Number of titles available: 52

Relation to the printed version: 20% complete, 60% abridged, 20% original

Sound/music: sound effects and music

Library discount: yes

Terms: 10% library discount

Genres: nonfiction

Replacement: No charge for damaged cassettes

Company focus: Writers of the land, the West, and natural history reading their own work.

Audio Press, recently purchased by Northword Press, has a wide assortment of short tapes, some of which are complete. The ones I have listened to have been excellent productions, and prices are reasonable. No longer distributed by Roberts Reinhart.

Audio Renaissance is a division of Cassette Productions Unlimited and produces and distributes mostly abridged audio books. Address: 5858 Wilshire

Boulevard, Suite 205, Los Angeles, CA 90036. Phone: 213-939-1840; FAX: 213-939-6436.

The Audio Store distributes the mostly short form and abridged products of Wisconsin Public Radio. Address: 821 University Avenue, Madison, WI 53706. Phone: 800-972-8346, 608-265-4548.

AudioBookCassettes
P. O. Box 3798
Estes Park, CO 80517
Sales: 800-537-9333; FAX 800-528-9888
Distributor

Number of titles available: 20,000+

Relation to the printed version: 25% complete, 75% abridged

Sound/music: sound effects and music and neither

Library discount: yes

Genres: adventure, classics, modern fiction, nonfiction, self-help, romance, Westerns, biographies, children's and YA, poetry and drama, religious, inspirational, science fiction, economics, history, and philosophy

Replacement: $6 per cassette plus shipping $.65; no charge for defective tapes

Shipping and billing: Add 4% for shipping

Company focus: As a distributor, we offer libraries a one-stop shopping service for abridged and unabridged audio books and a repackaging service, and we obtain replacement tapes for the libraries.

August House Audio
P. O. Box 3223
Little Rock, AR 72203-3223
501-372-5450, 800-284-8784; FAX 501-372-5579
Producer and distributor

Number of titles available: 30 approximate

Relation to the printed version: generally abridged

Sound/music: sound effects and music

Library discount: yes

Genres: traditional and revivalist storytellers

Replacement: $3 per cassette

Shipping and billing: freight prepaid by publisher

Distribution: We distribute nationally. Wholesalers such as Ingram and Baker and Taylor also carry our audio.

Company focus: Many of our artists are frequent guests at the National Storytelling Festival.

August House is a leading purveyor of storytelling tapes, some of which are derived from the annual National Storytelling Festival. Those tapes are some of the best live versions as they have enough audience noise to preserve the live feeling, but not enough to be distracting. Airpak.

Bantam Audio Publishing
1540 Broadway
New York, NY 10036
212-354-6500, 800-323-9872
Producer

Number of titles available: 250 approximate

Relation to the printed version: 10% complete, 90% abridged

Sound/music: sound effects and music

Library discount: yes

Terms: Contact publisher for information

Genres: adventure, modern fiction, nonfiction, self-help, Westerns, inspiration, business, and young adult fiction

Replacement: We are developing a policy to supply replacement cassettes for a low charge.

Distribution: Baker and Taylor, Ingram, and many more

Company focus: We focus on best-sellers on tape, published simultaneously with the hard-cover edition.

Bantam has only recently begun to produce complete audio.

Blackstone Audio Books
P. O. Box 969
Ashland, OR 97520
503-776-5179, 800-729-2665
Producer and distributor

Number of titles available: 450 approximate

Relation to the printed version: complete

Sound/music: neither

Library discount: yes

Terms: 10% discount on any purchase, more than 10 titles 15%, more than 100 titles 20%

Genres: adventure, classics, modern fiction, nonfiction, Westerns, and others

Replacement: free replacements for one year, $6 thereafter

Distribution: We are the primary distributors. However, approximately 12% of our annual sales occur through approximately one dozen distributors.

Company focus: Our title emphasis is on "books of content" as opposed to "best-sellers." While all other producers cater to those who want to be entertained, we target a customer who wants to learn and grow.

Blackstone Audio Books, formerly known as Classics on Tape, has been a leader in holding prices down while providing recordings of books that are more than entertainment. Originally its catalog was dominated by products from other companies, most of which lacked artistic finesse, but Blackstone is now recording most of its own work, to good effect. At one time the books were mostly classics, especially of a neoconservative bent, but the list now shows a much broader intellectual spectrum. Tape quality is high, but the technical quality of the recordings is sometimes slipshod. Bookpak.

Books in Motion
E. 9212 Montgomery, Suite 501
Spokane, WA 99206
509-922-1646, 800-752-3199; FAX 509-922-1445
Producer and distributor

Number of titles available: 300. We have recorded over 600 titles but retired those that were old or less popular.

Relation to the printed version: complete

Sound/music: neither

Library discount: yes

Terms: 10% on orders up to $299; 15% on $300-999; 20% on $1,000 and up; discounts are cumulative over time.

Genres: adventure, classics, modern fiction, non-fiction, self-help, romance, and Westerns

Replacement: Replacements are always free since 1980.

Distribution: Baker and Taylor, Audio Book Cassettes, Professional Media Services, Bodner and Associates

Company focus: We publish new manuscripts on tape. We have the world's largest selection of unabridged Westerns.

Books in Motion gained great visibility as a producer of classic fiction, utilizing the highest artistic and technical standards. Of late they have begun to emphasize recordings of unpublished and local authors, with mixed results. A good reading is a given, but sometimes the books are not as strong as they might be. Bookpak.

Books on Tape, Inc.
729 Farad St.
Costa Mesa, CA 92627
800-541-5525
Producer and distributor

Number of titles available: 2,500 approximate

Relation to the printed version: complete

Sound/music: neither

Library discount: yes

Terms: 20–30%

Genres: adventure, classics, modern fiction, nonfiction, self-help, romance, and Westerns

Replacement: Within one year, free replacement; after a year, $5 per cassette

Shipping and billing: Standard policies apply

Company focus: All tapes are unabridged, nondramatic, single-voice readings in award-winning classically designed albums.

Books on Tape is the largest and oldest audio book publisher. However, I find that its products vary wildly in quality. Some of the best titles are from independent, especially British, producers. Also, the company's prices are high, and the bibliographic information is often incomplete or inaccurate. These problems stem from a history as a renter of tapes to the public and from the many sources from which its tapes come. The very size of the organization makes it frustrating to deal with at times. Bookpak.

Bridge Audio
4751 Fountain Ave.
Los Angeles, CA 90029
800-722-1733, 800-843-7389 (CA)
Producer and distributor

Number of titles available: 17

Relation to the printed version: abridged

Sound/music: sound effects and music

Library discount: yes

Terms: One copy, 10% off retail; 2–5, 20%; 6–10, 30%; 11 and up, 33⅓%

Genres: self-help, Westerns, horror, and science fiction

Replacement: At original price unless defective; return entire product for replacement

Distribution: Ingram, Baker and Taylor

Company focus: Highest-quality, most-advanced technology is used on each recording, giving spectacular audio sound reproduction and years of service.

Brilliance Corp.
1810B Industrial Park Dr.
P. O. Box 887
Grand Haven, MI 49917
616-846-5256, 800-222-3225
Producer

Number of titles available: 150+

Relation to the printed version: complete

Sound/music: neither

Library discount: yes

Genres: adventure, classics, modern fiction, nonfiction, and romance

Replacement: Free

Distribution: All major distributors, including Ingram, Baker and Taylor, and so on

Company focus: Always unabridged

Brilliance has always been unafraid to innovate technically. Until recently its works were available only on multitrack versions, which must be played on a stereo machine or with an adaptor. Its library editions are not multitracked, however, and are a necessity for library use. Other technical innovations include data compression, which speeds up the reading without changing voice quality (in theory at least), and electronic manipulation of the sound to represent memories, phone voices, telepathic communication, and other special effects. Sometimes these work very well, and sometimes they are intrusive, though personal tastes vary. Brilliance uses lamentably cheap tape but offers free perpetual replacement. Bookpak.

Buckingham Classics
P. O. Box 597441
Chicago, IL 60625
312-338-7407, 800-354-7836
Producer

Number of titles available: 40

Relation to the printed version: 50% complete, 50% abridged

Sound/music: sound effects and music

Library discount: yes

Terms: Free shipping to libraries with each order

Genres: adventure, classics, nonfiction, romance, and Westerns

Replacement: $2 per cassette plus shipping

Shipping and billing: Net 30 days, free shipping with each order

Company focus: Our tapes are economically priced, $7.95 for one cassette, $12.95 for two, $15.95 for three.

Caedmon: see HarperAudio

Chivers North America/Chivers Audio Books
1 Lafayette Road
P. O. Box 1450
Hampton, NH 03842-0015
603-926-8744, 800-621-0182; FAX 603-929-3890
Producer and distributor

Number of titles available: 797

Relation to the printed version: complete

Sound/music: neither

Library discount: yes

Terms: 20% discount for standing orders; volume discount 10% or more on large orders; please inquire.

Genres: adventure, classics, modern fiction, nonfiction, romance, and Westerns

Replacement: $5 per cassette, postage included; defective tapes are replaced free at any time.

Shipping and billing: Prepaid orders are shipped free; otherwise, customer is charged for postage only (no handling charge).

Distribution: No other publisher distributes our titles; however, Chivers Audio Books may be ordered from any major library jobber such as Baker and Taylor.

Company focus: We only produce unabridged recordings, use professional actors and actresses, record in studios, and duplicate using Dolby system encoding. We have the largest selection of works by British authors of any popular audio publisher.

Chivers Audio Books, the leading British supplier of complete audio books, tends to record works that were quite popular (especially in Britain) a generation or so ago. Therefore, some of the titles are of interest and some are relatively unknown. The readings are usually full voice but down-played, which suits the title list well. The bookpak cases tend not to be as sturdy as some. Chivers now distributes Cover to Cover and Dercum audio books.

Christians Listening/Northstar Audio
P. O. Box 129
Van Wyck, SC 29744
803-283-2858, 800-522-2979; FAX 803-286-4151

Producer and distributor

Number of titles available: 300+

Relation to the printed version: complete

Sound/music: neither

Library discount: yes

Genres: adventure, classics, modern fiction, nonfiction, self-help, romance, Westerns, and Christian books

Replacement: $4 per cassette

These companies specialize in religious literature. Christians Listening's list is overtly fundamentalist, while Northstar has more general interest titles. Bookpak.

Cover to Cover is a very fine British audio company that specializes in classics; its products are solely distributed by Chivers North America.

Dercum Audio Inc.
P. O. Box 1425
West Chester, PA 19380
215-430-8889; FAX 215-430-8891
Producer and distributor

Number of titles available: 74

Relation to the printed version: complete

Sound/music: music between chapters or short stories

Library discount: yes

Terms: Inquire

Genres: adventure, classics, mystery, science fiction, and fantasy

Replacement: $3 per cassette

Distribution: Baker and Taylor, Ingram and Chivers Audio Books, American Wholesale Book Service, Walden, and Professional Media

Company focus: format includes short audio introduction giving some background on the author, story, and genre.

Dercum has an eclectic list with a lot of classics. The readings tend to be fully voiced and pretty good, but not exceptional. Bookpak.

Distribution Video & Audio
1060 Kapp Drive
Clearwater, FL 34625
800-321-9233
Distributor

Number of titles available: 300–450

Relation to the printed version: complete, abridged, and condensed

Sound/music: sound effects and music

Library discount: yes

Genres: adventure, classics, modern fiction, nonfiction, self-help, romance, and Westerns

Replacement: credit or exchange for defects

Shipping and billing: net 30 days, shipping UPS Ground

Distribution: approved distributors

Company focus: Audio is very affordable to libraries and ready for shelf display.

Dove Audio
301 North Canon Drive
Beverly Hills, CA 90210
310-273-7722, 800-345-9945
Producer

Number of titles available: 600

Relation to the printed version: 20% complete, 80% abridged

Sound/music: sound effects and music

Library discount: yes

Genres: adventure, classics, modern fiction, nonfiction, self-help, romance, Westerns, current biography, humor, and movie soundtracks

Replacement: $8 per tape

Distribution: wholesalers, retailers, etc.

Company focus: best-sellers read by celebrities

Dove is another specialist in abridged audio, who has begun to record complete books.

Dual Dolphin
224 Dedham St.
Norfolk, MA 02056
800-336-5746; FAX 508-384-6566

Dual Dolphin was formed by refugees from the breakup of G. K. Hall. They distribute Isis/Oasis Audio Books (formerly distributed by Recorded Books) in the United States and plan to begin original production.

Durkin Hayes Publishing Ltd.
One Colomba Drive
Niagara Falls, NY 14305
800-962-5200 (NY), 800-263-5244 (Canada); FAX 716-298-5607

Producer

Number of titles available: 250 approximate

Relation to the printed version: 30% complete, 70% abridged

Sound/music: neither

Library discount: yes

Terms: 10% discount on order of ten or more

Genres: adventure, classics, modern fiction, nonfiction, and Westerns

Replacement: $5 per tape

Shipping and billing: shipped UPS unless otherwise specified

Distribution: Baker and Taylor, Ingram

Company focus: We approach audio as a storyteller.

Durkin Hayes, based in Canada, specializes in very skillfully abridged and interpreted classic fiction. Bookpak.

G. K. Hall used to distribute Chivers Audio in the United States, but this is no longer the case, as of 1/1/93. Hall's titles are now distributed by Thorndike Press. Bookpak.

HarperAudio
1000 Keystone Industrial Park
Scranton, PA 18512
800-331-3761, 800-242-7737
Producer and distributor

Number of titles available: 1,100 approximate

Relation to the printed version: 20% complete, 80% abridged

Sound/music: sound effects and music

Library discount: no

Genres: classics, modern fiction, nonfiction, self-help, romance, Westerns, plays, business, children's, and mystery

Replacement: at original price

Distribution: Baker and Taylor, Ingram

Company focus: The Caedmon imprints offer 40 years of the classics, with many of the authors reading their own words.

Harper now distributes the Caedmon backlist, which includes many classic dramas and other short works.

High Windy Audio
P. O. Box 553
Fairview, NC 28732
800-637-8679

Producer

Number of titles available: 11

Relation to the printed version: complete

Sound/music: music

Library discount: no

Genres: children's and music

Replacement: none

Distribution: Baker and Taylor, Ingram, and lots more

Company focus: We do original storytelling (not from books) told by professional storytellers.

Isis/Oasis is a fine British producer of modern fiction distributed by Dual Dolphin.

JimCin Recording
P. O. Box 536
Portsmouth, RI 02871
800-538-3034
Producer and distributor

Number of titles available: 248

Relation to the printed version: 99% complete, 1% abridged

Sound/music: neither

Library discount: yes

Terms: straight 20%

Genres: adventure, classics, Westerns, and mystery

Replacement: free for one year, thereafter $5 per cassette

Company focus: Our focus is strictly classics—books that have stood the test of time and will be as popular now as 50 years from now.

JimCin, one of the earliest complete audio book producers, has failed to keep up with the stylistic innovations of competitors. Many of its unvoiced classic titles are available, sometimes more cheaply, from other producer/distributors.

Laubach Literacy: see New Readers Press

LibertyTree: Review and Catalog
134 Ninety-Eighth Ave.
Oakland, CA 94603
800-927-8733 (credit card orders only: MC, VISA, AmEx), 510-568-6047 (inquiries); FAX 510-568-6040

Producer and distributor

Number of titles available: 70 approximate

Relation to the printed version: 70% complete, 30% abridged

Sound/music: music

Library discount: no

Genres: classics, nonfiction, and self-help

Replacement: Defective cassette must be returned within ten days for replacement.

Shipping and billing: Schools and libraries to be billed. No COD orders. All orders require prepayment or purchase orders.

Company focus: topics pertaining to liberty

Listening Library
One Park Avenue
Old Greenwich, CT 06870
203-637-3616, 800-243-4504; FAX 203-698-1998
Producer and distributor

Number of titles available: 263 self-produced and 1,300 total

Relation to the printed version: complete. For over 35 years we have produced only unabridged recordings of classic and contemporary literature. However, we also invented an audio series called the "cliffhanger." These titles include word-for-word narration of a book up to a dramatic scene; then the cassette ends, with the narrator urging the readers to continue reading on their own to find out what happens next. This pioneer series has been very successful in the school market and retains the purity of the unabridged approach to audio.

Sound/music: Sound effects and music are included only in our recordings for very young children. Other than that we believe they detract from the spoken-word experience.

Library discount: no

Genres: classics, modern fiction, and children's

Replacement: lifetime free replacement

Shipping and billing: 6% to cover UPS, insurance, and shipping materials

Distribution: Our titles are widely available through over 100 quality educational catalog houses, educational paperback wholesalers, building-level distributors, and educational book clubs.

Company focus: Our focus always has been to produce and distribute the finest in literature-based media for children and adults. We offer over 1,300 titles. Our definition of literature-based is rather sharply focused by constant feedback from our customers, reviewers, authors, agents, publishers, and an in-house editorial board who read, listen to, and view every title offered in our catalog. We take the editorial viewpoint so nicely expressed by S. E. Hinton:

When asked if it was okay if people read anything as long as they were reading, she replied, "That is like a parent saying, 'My children eat junk food all day long, but at least they are eating.' "

Listening Library is the oldest and perhaps the largest children's audio publisher. Their material is first rate, but their prices are quite high. Bookpak.

Literate Ear Inc.
P. O. Box 29762
Elkins Park, PA 19117-9943
215-576-7709, 800-777-8327
Producer and distributor

Number of titles available: 34

Relation to the printed version: complete

Sound/music: neither

Library discount: yes

Terms: quantity discounts cumulative through year

Genres: adventure, modern fiction, nonfiction, and others

Replacement: $2 plus shipping per cassette

Company focus: Initially catered to libraries in cost, packaging, discounts. Now extending to retail distribution.

Literate Ear is a new company that has a short but varied list. Its productions are done by the reader on his own, and the results are sometimes less than state of the art in my experience. Bookpak.

Metacom Inc./Adventures in Cassettes/Rezound
5353N Nathan Lane
Plymouth, MN 55442
800-328-4818
Producer and distributor

Number of titles available: 900 approximate

Relation to the printed version: complete

Sound/music: sound effects and music

Library discount: no

Genres: Most titles are old-time radio shows and include the genres of adventure, classics, modern fiction, nonfiction, self-help, romance, and Westerns.

Replacement: If our fault, replace free of charge; if from use, at original price.

Company focus: In 1993, we will look at handling audio books. Right now our central focus is Old Time Radio, with some Self-Help and Music and Children's materials.

Mind's Eye
4 Commercial Blvd.
Novato, CA 94949
800-227-2020, 415-883-7701
Producer and distributor

Number of titles available: 300 approximate

Relation to the printed version: 10% complete, 90% abridged

Sound/music: sound effects and music

Library discount: no

Genres: adventure, classics, nonfiction, and Westerns

Replacement: $7.95 per cassette, $1 for libraries

Company focus: Uniquely produced cassettes that are dramatized, not read. Read-along books.

Mind's Eye was well known as a producer of excellent radio dramatizations, but now concentrates on distributing high-quality audio of many types. Bookpak.

New Readers Press is the publishing division of Laubach Literacy International. They publish and distribute audio and other instructional materials for adult and young adult new readers. New Readers Press, P. O. Box 888, Syracuse, NY 13210, 800-448-8878.

Newman Audio: see Audio Partners

Northstar Audio: see Christians Listening

Northword Press: see Audio Press

Penguin/HighBridge Audio, a producer/distributor, is a coming player in abridged and short-form audio. The company distributes the productions of Minnesota Public Radio, including works by Garrison Keillor and a number of name authors. It also distributes the products of Wireless and other, mostly public-radio materials. Address: Order/New Accounts/Penguin USA, Box 120, 120 Woodbine Avenue, Bergenfield, NJ 07621. Phone: 800-526-0275, 800-331-4624; FAX 800-227-9604.

Poets' Audio Center
6925 Willow St. NW #201
Washington, DC 20012
800-366-9105

Distributor

Number of titles available: 523

Relation to the printed version: selected poems chosen from many volumes

Sound/music: sound effects and music

Library discount: yes, negotiable

Terms: $500 minimum order for discount

Genres: poetry

Replacement: Varies by producer. We are sensitive to the need for replacements and try to provide them at our cost.

Shipping and billing: FOB our office; billing net 30 days

Company focus: We are the only comprehensive distributor of poetry recordings, representing some 39 producers' titles.

Poets' Audio Center and Watershed Tapes have the same address and phone number.

Publishers Group West: see Audio Partners

The Publishing Mills
1680 N. Vine Street #1016
Los Angeles, CA 90028
800-722-8346, 213-467-7831; FAX 213-467-0661
Producer

Number of titles available: 50 approximate

Relation to the printed version: 20% complete, 80% abridged

Sound/music: sound effects and music very occasionally used

Library discount: yes

Terms: free freight

Genres: adventure, classics, modern fiction, nonfiction, romance, Westerns, and humor

Replacement: Defectives replaced at no charge. For wear, we have no policy yet.

Company focus: We try to offer a well-rounded selection of quality books, with an eye toward originality in the underlying work or toward other special merit (for example, *Backlash* by Susan Faludi).

The Reader's Chair
860 Chappell Rd.
Hollister, CA 95023
408-636-1296

Producer

Number of titles available: 4

Relation to the printed version: complete

Sound/music: neither

Library discount: no

Genres: adventure and modern fiction

Replacement: Free if defective on first playback. If damaged, $4 per cassette (includes postage).

Company focus: We sell unabridged adult fiction audio in attractive vinyl cases at an affordable price.

The Chair specializes in two voice recordings of Dean Koontz's horror fantasies. The production quality is very high. Bookpak.

Recorded Books, Inc.
270 Skipjack Road
Prince Frederick, MD 20678
800-638-1304, 410-535-5590; FAX 410-535-5499
Producer and distributor

Number of titles available: 750 approximate

Relation to the printed version: complete

Sound/music: neither

Library discount: yes

Genres: adventure, classics, modern fiction, nonfiction, and Westerns

Replacement: One-year library warranty. Non-warranty library replacement currently is $5.95, with postage included.

Company focus: Recorded Books, Inc., offers a full range of library services. Recorded Books, Inc., is a sole-source company.

Recorded Books is the second oldest of the complete audio book publishers, following Books on Tape. The quality of its productions is consistently very high in every way. However, sometimes the readers tend to take the books they present a little too seriously for my taste, which often results in a slow, rather underwhelming reading. For some unknown reason the company uses an order number rather than an ISBN to identify their titles. One advantage of this practice is that the first two numbers in a tape order number give the year of the tape's release. Bookpak.

**Redding's Bestseller Audiobook Superstores
    and Mail Rental "Listen Update"**
2302 North Scottsdale Rd.
Scottsdale, AZ 85257
602-481-0074, 800-BESTSELLER

Distributor

Number of titles available: 11,000 approximate

Relation to the printed version: complete and abridged

Sound/music: Some have sound effects, and some have music.

Library discount: yes

Terms: 10% off for larger orders, over $500

Genres: adventure, classics, modern fiction, nonfiction, self-help, romance, and Westerns

Replacement: at original price

Shipping and billing: net 30

Company focus: world's largest selection of audiobooks

Redding's sells through an eclectic catalog, which features an interesting review column by Bennet Pomerantz.

Ride With Me
P. O. Box 1324
Bethesda, MD 20817
800-752-3195, 301-299-7817
Producer and distributor

Number of titles available: 23

Relation to the printed version: These are original works for audio.

Sound/music: neither

Library discount: no

Genres: nonfiction, history, and travel

Replacement: if tape broken by customer, 40%; if tape misbehaves, free.

Distribution: In bookstores and by Baker and Taylor

Ride With Me is unique among audio books producers in that its products are designed for travelers to listen to along interstate highways. These tapes are produced by Flo Gibson's AudioBook Contractors.

Roberts Reinhart: see Audio Press

Seven Wolves Publishing
8928 National Blvd.
Los Angeles, CA 90034
800-852-2474 (airpak)
Producer and distributor

Number of titles available: 3

Relation to the printed version: complete

Sound/music: sound effects and music

Library discount: yes

Terms: on order of two or more, 20% discount

Genres: modern fiction and nonfiction

Replacement: $7 per cassette

Shipping and billing: Libraries pay shipping, net 30.

Distribution: Ingram, Baker and Taylor, Pacific Pipeline, Golden Lee, Audio Partners, and AudioBookCassettes

Sounds True Catalog
735 Walnut St.
Boulder, CO 80302
800-333-9185; FAX 303-449-9226
Customer Service: 303-449-6229
Producer and distributor

Number of titles available: 250 approximate

Relation to the printed version: no printed versions

Sound/music: music

Library discount: yes

Terms: Discount depends on number of titles ordered. Less than 10, no discount; 10–19 titles, 10%; 20 or more, 20%.

Genres: self-help, psychology, and spirituality

Replacement: Will replace any cassette at any time for any reason.

Company focus: We focus solely on tapes that help people in their everyday lives. All our material on tape is original work.

Spencer Library
116–200 Village Blvd.
Princeton, NJ 00540
609-520-7955, 800-934-6000
Producer and distributor

Number of titles available: 6

Relation to the printed version: complete

Sound/music: sound effects and music

Library discount: yes

Terms: 20% discount; net 30

Genres: classics

Replacement: Free for defective tapes; $1.50 per cassette plus shipping for wear.

Spencer may represent the future. Expert reader-actors, original electronic scores, and top-quality recording and tape make their productions special. Every library should have all six of their titles. Their titles once were and soon will again be available on compact disc. Bookpak. Also they will soon be available on CD-ROM for the Sony Data DiscMan.

Spine-Tingling Press
P. O. Box 186
Agoura Hills, CA 91376
818-889-1575
Producer and distributor

Number of titles available: 12

Relation to the printed version: complete

Sound/music: sound effects and music

Library discount: yes

Terms: Library P.O. 20–40%, 30-Day terms

Genres: nonfiction, dark fantasy, and horror

Replacement: Within one year at no cost; after one year at 50% of original
  price.

Distribution: Baker and Taylor, Ingram, New Leaf

Spoken Arts, one of the pioneers in the field, is now owned by School Book Fairs. Their backlist of short-form audio is still mostly available. Address: 801 94th Ave. North, Suite 100, St. Petersburg, FL 33702. Phone: 800-326-4090, 813-578-7600.

Stemmer House Publishers
2627 Caves Bldg.
Owings Mills, MD 21117
301-363-3690
Producer

Number of titles available: 4

Relation to the printed version: complete

Sound/music: sound effects and music

Library discount: yes

Genres: classics

Replacement: at original price

Distribution: Baker and Taylor and Ingram

Company focus: We only record our own published books, if they lend themselves to recording.

Sterling Audio
P. O. Box 159
Thorndike, ME 04986
207-948-2962, 800-223-6121
Producer and distributor

Number of titles available: 40; ongoing program of five titles per quarter

Relation to the printed version: complete

Sound/music: neither

Library discount: yes

Terms: Standing-order discount is 25% with free freight. Normal purchases, 10% discount.

Genres: adventure, classics, modern fiction, and romance

Replacement: within one year, free; thereafter $6 per cassette

Shipping and billing: Free freight with standing order. Customer pays all others.

Distribution: Library Jobbers, Baker and Taylor, and others

Company focus: We try harder.

Sterling distributes selected titles from the Chivers list, which are not available from Chivers Audio Books. The company tends to obtain some of the best productions, with titles of special interest to U.S. listeners. New titles from Spencer Library in production. Bookpak.

Tapes for Readers
5078 Fulton St., N.W.
Washington, DC 20016
202-362-4585
Producer and distributor

Number of titles available: 150 approximate

Relation to the printed version: interviews

Sound/music: neither

Library discount: 40% on 10+ items

Terms: discount on orders of five or more

Genres: modern fiction and nonfiction

Replacement: if defective, free within 30 days

Shipping and billing: We use cheapest rate unless otherwise requested.

Distribution: American Audio Prose Library

Company focus: We do interviews of outstanding contemporary figures especially authors, not readings or dramatizations.

Thorndike Press
100 Front St.
P. O. Box 500
Riverside, NJ 08075-7500
800-257-5755; FAX 800-562-1272
Producer and distributor

Number of titles available: 821

Relation to the printed version: complete

Sound/music: neither

Library discount: yes

Terms: 15% discount on five or more titles

Genres: adventure, classics, modern fiction, nonfiction, romance, and Westerns

Replacement: Thorndike will replace defective cassettes for free within 365 days of purchase or receipt; after 365 days (1 year) will replace any cassette for $6.

Distribution: Baker and Taylor, AudioBookCassettes, and Professional Media, as well as other jobbers

Company focus: We feature American best-sellers and popular fiction.

Thorndike Press distributes titles and replacement tapes for G. K. Hall, Story Sound Audio Books, and Ulverscroft Soundings. Sterling Audio is part of Thorndike but separate.

Watershed Tapes
6925 Willow St., NW #201
Washington, DC 20012
202-722-9105, 800-366-9105; FAX 202-722-9106
Producer

Number of titles available: 165

Relation to the printed version: Poems are complete, but tapes rarely duplicate books in terms of selections.

Sound/music: Included only if chosen by the poet as part of the performance.

Library discount: yes

Terms: Standing orders, 30% discount; orders for $300 or more subject to discount.

Genres: poetry (read by the poet)

Replacement: $2 service charge at any time

Shipping and billing: FOB our office (free shipping on large orders). Billing: net 30.

Distribution: Inland Book Co., Bookpeople, Baker and Taylor, The Audio Buff

Company focus: We are the largest producer of poets' recordings (and virtually the only active one). Best-sellers include Gary Snyder, Sharon Olds, May Sarton, Galway Kinnell, and Allen Ginsberg.

Watershed Tapes and Poets' Audio Center have the same address and phone number.

Weston Woods is a producer and distributor of high-quality children's audio books. Address: Weston Woods, Weston, CT 06883-1199. Phone: 800-243-5020; in Connecticut, call collect 226-3355; FAX 203-226-3818.

Williamson Distributors Inc.
4305-B Norman Bridge Rd.
Montgomery, AL 36105
205-281-2007, 800-AUDIOVIDEO (800-283-4684)
Producer and distributor

Number of titles available: 40,000+ approximate

Relation to the printed version: 20% complete, 80% abridged

Sound/music: sound effects and music

Library discount: yes

Genres: adventure, classics, modern fiction, nonfiction, self-help, romance, and Westerns

Replacement: at cost

Wireless Audio Collection: see Penguin/Highbridge

Yellow Moon Press, a producer and distributor of storytelling tapes, offers more titles and much more variety than does August House. Address: P. O. Box 1316, Cambridge, MA 02238. Phone: 617-776-2230; FAX 617-776-8246.

ZBS Foundation
RR 1, Box 1201
Fort Edward, NY 12828
800-395-2549
Producer and distributor

Number of titles available: 25

Relation to the printed version: complete

Sound/music: sound effects and music

Library discount: yes

Genres: adventure and science fiction

Replacement: at original price

Distribution: Baker and Taylor

ZBS makes a few of its newer titles available on compact disc. Their titles are all original radio scripts with excellent aural variety and quality, with sci-fi/ fantasy story lines.

Bibliography

Annichiarico, M. (1992). Playing for time: The delicate art of abridging audiobooks. *Library Journal, 117* (19), 41–44.

Annichiarico, M. (1992). Spoken word audio: The fastest growing library collection. *Library Journal, 116* (9), 36–38.

Asheim, Lester. (1987). *The Reader-viewer-listener.* Viewpoint Series, no. 18. Washington, D.C.: Library of Congress Center for the Book.

Audio bestsellers, January 1993. (1993). *Publishers Weekly, 240* (1), 31.

Audiovisual Committee, Public Library Association. (1975). *Recommendations for audiovisual materials and services for small and medium-sized public libraries.* Chicago: American Library Association.

Ballard, T. H. (1986). *The failure of resource sharing in public libraries and alternative strategies for service.* Chicago: American Library Association.

Bauer, K. & Drew, R. (1991). *Lesson plan book for the whole language and literature-based classroom.* Cypress, CA: Creative Teaching Press.

Behrens, T. (1991, July) [Interview with P. Hoffman].

Bliss, B. A. (1979). Help for unsuccessful readers: Recorded reading program gives pleasure and success. *Wisconsin Library Bulletin, 75,* 79–82.

Boyle, T. (1991, August) [Interview with P. Hoffman].

Briggs, S. & Sorrell, G. (1991). *How to rescue at-risk students.* (2nd ed.) (Cassette Recording) Clifton, VA: Sound Reading Associates.

Burr, S. (1991, August) [Interview with P. Hoffman].

Carbo, M. (1989). *How to record books for maximum reading gains.* Roslyn Heights, NY: National Reading Styles Institute, Inc.

Carbo, M. (1981). Making books talk to children. *The Reading Teacher, 35,* 186–189.

Carter, B. & Abrahamson, R. F. (1991). Nonfiction in a read-aloud program. *Journal of Reading, 34,* 638–642.

Comer, M. (1991, July) [Interview with P. Hoffman].

Conte, R. & Humphreys, R. (1989). Repeated readings using audiotaped material enhances oral reading in children with reading difficulties. *Journal of Communication Disorders, 22,* 65–79.

Davis, D. (1991, March) [Interview with P. Hoffman].

Dunn, R. & Dunn, K. (1993). *Teaching secondary students through their individual learning styles.* Boston, MA: Allyn & Bacon.

Estelle, D. (1990, May 30) [Letter to P. Hoffman].

Forster, P. & Doyle, B. A. (1989). Teaching listening skills to students with attention deficit disorders. *Teaching Exceptional Children, 21* (2), 20–22.

Hecht, D. (1992, September 30) [Letter to C. Osteyee].

Hoffman, P. (1992). Book Sounds. *Wilson Library Bulletin, 67* (1), 75–77.

Hoffman, P. (1992). Book Sounds. *Wilson Library Bulletin, 67* (3), 59–61.

Hoffman, P. (1991). A change of voice: The art of the spoken word. *Library Journal, 116* (19), 39–43.

Hoffman, P. (1992). Covert entry: The backdoor electronic revolution. *Wilson Library Bulletin, 67* (3), 35–37.

Johnston, D. F. (1982). *Copyright Handbook,* 2nd ed. New York: R. R. Bowker Co.

Kearns, K. (1985). The forgotten medium—Are we too visually dependent? *NASSP Bulletin, 69* (480), 45–49.

Lande, N. (1991). Toward the electronic book. *Publishers Weekly, 238* (42), 28–9.

Lewis, R. (1991, July) [Interview with P. Hoffman].

Muller, F. (1991, July) [Interview with P. Hoffman].

Prillaman, S. (1992). Whole language and its effect on the school library media center. *North Carolina Libraries, 50,* 161–4.

Publishers Weekly. (1991). *Audio market study phase II—Among libraries.* NY: Cahners Publisher's Market Research Dept.

Reilly, P. M. (1991, July 11). The sounds of war: DCC vs. minidisc. *Wall Street Journal,* p. B1.

Reissman, R. (1992). *Teaching tips for using audio cassettes in literature classes.* NY: Penguin USA.

Rickelman, R. J. & Henk, W. A. (1990). Children's literature and audio/visual technologies. *The Reading Teacher, 43,* 682–3.

Stubbs, B. (Ed.) (1992, Summer). *Trainer Touchstone* newsletter. Syracuse, NY: Laubach Literacy Action, *9,* 1–8.

Sumner, J. (1991, May 27). The voices that bring books to life. *The Dallas Morning News,* p. C1, C7.

Thurber, M. (Ed.) (1990). *The listening road to literacy.* Old Greenwich, CT: Listening Library, Inc.

Trentman, H. (1991, July) [Interview with P. Hoffman].

Words on cassette: Combining Meckler's Words on Tape with Bowker's 'On Cassette'. (1992). New Providence, NJ: R. R. Bowker.

Index

ABOUT THE CONTRIBUTORS

PRESTON HOFFMAN is the "Book Sounds" columnist for *Wilson Library Bulletin* and author of "A Change of Voice: The Art of the Spoken Word" (*Library Journal* [116, 19], 39–43) and a monograph on audio books, "Occasional Papers #184" (University of Illinois Press). He holds an M. A. in speech communications and English from Columbia University and is the extension services librarian for the Burke County Public Library in North Carolina.

CAROL H. OSTEYEE received a doctorate in education from Columbia University and teaches in the Burke County, North Carolina, public schools. She is the author of *Critical Thinking Model and Handbook* (United Way of America, 1992). Her interest in curricula innovations, especially whole language, led to her research in the use of audio books in education.

KATHI SIPPEN has been Audiovisual Librarian at the Durham Public Library, Durham, North Carolina for the last eight years. She is a member of the audio-visual committee of the North Carolina Library Association.